Every House Had a Secret

Growing up in the shadow of our father's secrets

Written by: LK Menzies

Contributions by: RD Peterson

LKM Story House, LLC

Author and Contributors Note:

This is a true story. Every chapter is rooted in real events and lived experiences.

The kind of truth that doesn't fade with time.

Although we removed names and adapted some events, the struggle, resilience, and fight to rise above abuse are profoundly real.

We wrote "Every House Had a Secret" not to relive the past but to transform it. Into healing. Into something someone else might pick up and realize…they're not alone.

There is life after fear.

There is joy after trauma.
There is "freedom"—waiting for you to take it.

Thank you for walking through these pages with us.

If this book finds you at the right time,

Then maybe, just maybe…
We all found home.

About the Author and Contributor:

LK Menzies and RD Peterson are Storytellers united by blood, experience, and unbreakable resilience.

Together, they have transformed their shared history of hardship and survival into a powerful memoir that brings light to the shadows of family trauma. Raised in small-town Ohio, their journey has been one of navigation silence, confronting truth, and choosing freedom.

Each house had a secret.

Prologue

There are some houses that look perfectly normal from the outside—neatly trimmed lawns, curtains drawn just right, maybe even a flag fluttering in the breeze. Ours was one of those. On Vine Street, the truth didn't scream. It whispered.

Inside, the walls remembered everything. Throughout the room, the sound of slammed doors echoed. The spark of matches. The cry of a child holding still, hoping not to be noticed. Love wasn't the kind you read about in storybooks. It was a transaction, a performance, a punishment.

Before we moved to our next home, the ground was already shaking. There were too many babies too fast, too many secrets tucked under beds, too many rules that changed with the wind. Our father ruled like a shadow there, but not fully seen. You didn't look him in the eye. You didn't ask questions. You didn't eat the cherries.

By the time we arrived at our next house, something in all of us had already splintered. What happened to my oldest sister haunted her. My brother learned to run. And me? I learned how to disappear inside myself and reappear when it was safe.

But no one stays invisible forever.

This is the story of what happened inside those houses, how terror dressed itself as routine, how four children survived what should have destroyed them, and how sometimes the smallest act of defiance—like taking the blame for a cherry — can become the first step toward freedom.

We never meant it to be a horror story. But it became one.

And now my brother and I are ready to tell it.

Chapter 1

Three Days Later

Betrayal...

Before there was a wedding, there was Beulah.

She was the one my dad promised forever to. His fiancée. The woman he was supposed to marry. The one whose pictures would later haunt the walls of our house. Beulah wore the ring. She had the plans, the dress, the date marked on the calendar. She thought she knew who he was and what their future life would look like.

But Beulah didn't know about my mom. Not at first.

My mom was sixteen when she got pregnant.

She was still a child—barely through childhood herself—navigating a world that didn't leave room for innocence. My dad was older. He knew what he was doing. And he knew what getting her pregnant would mean. In that time, in that place, it wasn't a mistake. It was a trap with no easy way out.

When Beulah found out, she did the only thing she could.

She left.

One week before the wedding, Beulah broke off the engagement. She wouldn't marry a man who had gotten another girl pregnant. Maybe she still loved him. She may have been angry. Maybe she was heartbroken. But she knew enough to walk away. And for that, I'll always respect her. She saw the beginning of a storm and didn't wait to see how bad it would get.

But my mother didn't have that choice.

Pregnant at sixteen, she felt her childhood was over and faced confusion alone.

She had nowhere to go, no one to lean on, except for the man whose promises were already shattered. My mother was trapped in a whirlwind of expectations and social dictates, her choices stolen before she could understand what they meant. She didn't get to choose love; she chose survival. And survival meant stepping into Beulah's abandoned shoes, knowing full well that they would never fit.

So that's what happened.

My mom turned seventeen. Then three days after the wedding, she gave birth to my sister.

That should have been a time of joy, of rest, of celebration. But it was the start of a sentence. A life she hadn't chosen, bound to a man who blamed her for everything. My mom was a child, holding a child, married to a man still mourning the one who left him.

He made sure she knew it.

Beulah may have been gone, but her shadow moved in with us.

My dad punished my mother in the most bitter, deliberate way—by turning Beulah into a ghost who lived on every wall. He put pictures of her all over the house. Framed and unframed. Tucked into books. Pinned to cork boards. Stuffed in drawers. On the mirror in the bathroom. One on the fridge, and one on the inside of the cabinet door, so my mother would see it every time she reached for a plate.

He didn't hide them. He wanted my mom to see. Wanted her to feel it.

"This is who I should've married."

"This is what I lost because of you."

The message was obvious. Constant. Unforgiving.

My mother never talked back. What could she say? She was seventeen, with a newborn in her arms, living in a house that wasn't a home. She cooked. cleaned. fed a baby while pretending she didn't see the eyes of another woman staring at her from the corner of every room.

She stayed quiet. But there was sadness.

We saw it in the way her shoulders slumped when she picked up Beulah's photo off the floor. The way she would pause at the stove, eyes locked on nothing, lost in a thought too heavy to speak. The way she tucked her hair behind her ears with shaking hands.

She never had time to be a teenager. Never went to a prom. Never went a graduation. Someone stole her future, replacing it with dirty diapers and a man who wished she didn't exist.

My father never struck her with fists.
But he didn't need to.
He broke through to her with reminders.

Beulah became more than a person—she became a weapon.

He held up her beauty like a blade, compared her grace to my mother's exhaustion, her freedom to my mom's shackles. It wasn't enough to make my mother stay—he needed her to suffer. To carry the weight of his regret like a second child.

And she did.

Day after day. Week after week. Year after year.

But she kept going.

She raised my sister in that house, under the eyes of a woman who had escaped, while she herself stayed behind. She fed bottles under pictures. Rocked a baby to sleep beneath the gaze of a girl who had once worn a ring that now sat in a drawer with dust and spite.

Eventually, she would have more children. My siblings and me. She would fold laundry, pack lunches, clean floors. Building a life from the wreckage of another woman's departure, she would teach us how to be strong even while her own strength was fading.

And Beulah? We never met her.

But we knew her name.

From those fading photographs with curled corners and yellowing tape, we knew her face. We knew she had walked away from the man who became our nightmare. We knew she'd been free—something our mother had never been.

I wonder if Beulah ever thought about us.
About the girl who took her place.
About the baby born three days later.

I wonder if she ever imagined what became of the life she almost had.

Sometimes I envy her.
Not because she left him—but because she *could*.

My mom never had that luxury.

She didn't get to choose love.
She didn't get to build a dream.
Someone else's broken promises fell to her, and she received the blame for the consequences.

Despite that, she stayed.
Still, she mothered.
Still, she endured.

Even as the pictures watched her from every wall.

Chapter 2

Raggedy Ann

Discarded...

He didn't want her.

That much was clear from the beginning.
Without whispering. Not hidden. Not subtle.
He didn't like her. He didn't bond with her. Didn't
even try.

She was born just three days after they forced him
into marriage. Not because of love, not because of
joy, but because my mother was sixteen and
pregnant and alone. The wedding was damage
control. The birth was a consequence. And from
that moment on, my sister was the living proof of
everything he resented.

He never said her name with affection. Never
picked her up with gentleness. When he looked at
her, it was as if he saw a mistake he couldn't undo.
And when he touched her, it wasn't with care, it
was with disdain.

Our house was already suffocating. The walls held
too many secrets. The air was thick with control

and silence. And in the middle of all that sat my sister, just a baby—too small to understand why glares answered her cries, why people ignored her giggles, and why her father looked right through her as though she weren't even there.

But she was there.

And one day, he made sure she knew just how unwanted she really was.

She'd been crying. Perhaps she was hungry. Maybe she was tired. Maybe she just needed to be held the way babies do, the way they're supposed to be. But my dad didn't believe in softness. He believed in power. In control. In making a point.

He stormed into the room, his anger boiling over like it always did when reality didn't bend to his will. My sister was in my mother's arms. Still small, still fragile. Still needing protection from a world, she was barely part of.

And in a flash—without warning—he grabbed her.

My mother screamed, pleaded, tried to hold on. But it happened too fast. His hands yanked her tiny body from my mother's arms, and with a motion as cruel as it was casual, he *threw* her.

Not gently.

Not into her crib like a parent might toss a giggling toddler onto soft blankets.

No, he threw her as if she were weightless. Like she was a toy. Like she didn't matter.

She flew like a Raggedy Ann doll—limp, helpless, fragile. Her body struck the crib with a thud that still echoes in my mother's mind, years later. My sister didn't even cry right away. Just gasped— stunned. Then the sobs came. Loud. Broken. Frightened.

My mother was shaking. She rushed to the crib, scooped her up, checked every inch of her body for injuries while trying to hide her own terror. Somehow, she wasn't visibly hurt. No bruises. No broken bones. Just a baby who had already learned what it meant to be disposable.

A fracture occurred inside her.

Something that doesn't leave you.

There are things that children carry long before they have words to describe them. My sister carried within her the knowledge that she was unwanted. She was born into a house where love was conditional, and she had already failed the test. That her father—a man who was supposed to protect her—saw her as an object of regret.

And my mother? She carried guilt.

She couldn't stop it.
She saw it all.
The moment her child flew from her arms, she realized just how little power she had.

She didn't leave him that day. Where could she have gone? Seventeen years old, holding a baby in her arms, with nowhere to turn and no one to help. The world didn't come running to save girls like her. Not then. Maybe never.

So, she stayed.
And made herself small.
And tried to protect her child in all the quiet ways a woman with no power learns to do.

But how do you shield a child from a man who lives in the same house? From a father who looks at her and sees a cage instead of a gift?

You can't.

So, my sister learned. Early. Painfully. Quietly.

She grew up in the shadow of that moment— thrown like a toy, discarded like an inconvenience. And while the world moved on, taking school pictures and celebrating birthdays and continuing life, that memory weighed heavily on her.

The flight and its underlying message declared, *"You are not wanted."*

She wasn't the only one he hurt, but she was the first. The one who taught the rest of us what to expect. Avoiding anger is possible through these methods. How to stay invisible. How to recognize when something was about to boil over. She taught us how to read the room—not with our eyes, but with our fear.

And years later, when we tried to talk about it, the truth hung between us like fog.

"I remember him throwing her," my mom would say, voice barely above a whisper. "She was so little… I thought he'd killed her."

But he didn't.

He didn't break her body. He did something even worse.

He taught her from the very start that the person who should have loved her most didn't even like her. And that knowledge? It shaped her. It curled around her spirit like a bruise no one could see.

That moment was just one of many. But it was the first.
The warning shot.

The line drawn in the air.
The day my sister learned what it felt like to be a
rag doll in the hands of a man who didn't see her
as human.

And still—somehow—she survived.

A laugh burst from her. She loved. She grew.
But the pain never left.
Because how could it?

You don't forget the first time you realize you're
not safe in your own father's arms.
You don't forget being thrown like you weigh
nothing.
You don't forget crying in a crib, not just because
it hurt—but because it *meant something*.

It meant *you didn't matter*.

And that's a wound that no one ever sees.
But it bleeds all the same.

Chapter 3

Nature vs. Nurture

Origin…

People say that inheritance and experience shape children. But sometimes, it's not one or the other. Sometimes, it's the violence of both colliding inside a person until something breaks.

For my father, it began the day he came home from school and found his mother dead.

He was only seven years old.

A small boy in scuffed shoes, walking home down the gravel path with a heavy book bag and a head full of first-grade thoughts—maybe about lunch, maybe about a spelling test, maybe just about seeing his mother again. Because even if he didn't know it yet, she was his entire world. The one who packed his sandwiches, tucked him in at night, ran her hand through his hair when he had nightmares. The one stable, soft thing in his life.

He walked through the yard as always, pushing the gate open with a squeak that should have brought her to the porch. She always met him there. She always smiled. He always waved.

But the porch was empty.

So, he walked farther, calling her name.

And that's when he saw her.

She was lying near the fence, slumped in the grass, arms sprawled awkwardly, the lawn mower tipped beside her like a dropped toy. Her dress moved slightly in the breeze. But her body didn't.

He didn't understand at first.

He dropped his bag. Ran to her. Thought maybe she was resting. Maybe she'd fallen. Maybe she'd wake up.

But her eyes didn't open.
Her chest didn't rise.
Her fingers were stiff.

There was no blood. Just silence. A thick, awful kind of silence that swallows everything. It pressed against his ears until he thought they might burst. The air felt still. He reached for her hand. Shook it. Called her name again and again until his voice cracked.

That's when the scream came.

It sounded so raw it didn't sound human. A child's voice breaking under the weight of a truth too big for a seven-year-old heart.

A faulty wire had electrocuted her on the electric fence. The very thing meant to protect their property had killed her. No warning. No mercy. With one jolt, she collapsed there in the yard, just minutes before her boy came home.

Neighbors came running. Someone called the police. Someone else took my father inside and tried to hold him, but he just stared out-wide-eyed and hollow. As if they had buried a part of him alongside her, even before lowering her into the ground.

After that, the world changed.

He changed.

He stopped smiling. Stopped laughing. Stopped being a boy. That's what the adults said. He wasn't angry—just *gone*. His eyes always looked far away, like he was still standing in that yard, waiting for her to sit up, waiting for it all to be a mistake.

But it wasn't a mistake. It was the beginning.

Because no one helped him heal. No one sat him down and told him it was okay to cry, or that death wasn't his fault. His father—grieving in his own silent, hard way—expected him to move on. To "be a man." To grow up faster than any child ever should.

So, he did.

He locked the pain deep inside himself. Turned grief into silence. His fear became out of control. And maybe that's when the foundation cracked— when the boy who needed love learned that emotions were dangerous, that vulnerability was weakness, that no one was coming to save him.

And that boy eventually became a man.
And that man became my father.

A father who didn't know how to comfort.
Who didn't hold his children with tenderness?
Who didn't comfort us when we were scared, because he himself had received no comfort.
Who punished instead of protected, silenced instead of listened?

And when he raged, when he lashed out, when he haunted the house with his mood and his voice and his bitterness, we wondered why.

We didn't know the story then. We knew only the man he had become.

It wasn't until much later that we learned about the yard. About the body. About the seven-year-old boy who came home from school and found his mother lying lifeless in the grass.

That story doesn't excuse what came next. But it explains something. It offers context, not justification. Although pain may explain a person's path, it doesn't absolve the choices they make when they reach adulthood.

My father had a choice. He had chances. He had a family of his own.
And instead of breaking the cycle, he became the storm.

Maybe he thought cruelty was protection.
Maybe he thought control was love.
Maybe he thought if he kept everything locked down—his emotions, his family, his world—he would never have to feel helpless again.

But in trying to escape the helplessness of that moment in the yard, he became the very thing that wounded him—a source of fear for his children.

He used to tell my mother he didn't enjoy talking about his childhood. That it was "done," "over," "useless to revisit." But I wonder if he thought about her every day. If the image of her lying in the grass was the last gentle thing he ever remembered before the anger took root.

Sometimes I think about that boy. Not the man he became. The boy.

The one who dropped his school bag.
The one who ran barefoot across the yard.
The one who saw his mother lying in the grass and didn't yet understand what death was.

I feel for him. I do. He didn't deserve that moment. No child does.

But we didn't deserve what he became either.

Maybe that's the cruel twist of nature and nurture—how one moment can shape a soul, and how that soul, unhealed, can shatter others.

He lost his mother behind a fence.
And in a way, we lost ours to him.

Chapter 4

What He Took Without Lifting a Hand

Power...

There are bruises you can't see. Wounds that never show up in photographs. Scars that live not on skin, but in silence. My father never hit my mother—not with fists. But he broke her all the same. Slowly. Strategically. By using words. With shame. Such tight control left no room for air.

She had only a eighth-grade education.

Not because she wasn't bright, but because life didn't give her time to be a child. She had to quit school to care for her younger brothers' babies clinging to her hips while she wiped noses, cleaned floors, and learned how to raise a family before she ever had one of her own.

She never got to dream. Never had a moment to ask, "What do I want?" It was always about what everyone else needed. She was the caretaker, the helper, the invisible glue that held everyone else together. So, when my father came along—older, louder, full of false promises—he didn't see her innocence. He saw an opportunity.

She was Sixteen when she got pregnant. seventeen when they married. She went from raising her siblings to raising her own child without skipping a beat. No wedding shower. No honeymoon. He treated her like a burden, and a crib sat in a room she hadn't decorated.

From the start, he picked at her like a scab.

He mocked her reading, corrected her grammar in front of others, and laughed when she stumbled over words. When she got nervous, she'd stutter— and he'd mimic it, cruelly and without shame. "Use your words," he'd snap, as if she hadn't spent a lifetime swallowing them.

He never let her forget how "uneducated" she was.

He made sure she knew she didn't measure up. He didn't listen to himself. Not to his past. Not to the woman he once planned to marry before the pregnancy "ruined everything." Beulah's name lingered in the house like stale perfume. Her picture sat in drawers and shelves as a reminder: *You were never supposed to be here.*

My mother rarely raised her voice. She had learned early that compliance was safer than resistance.

But that didn't mean she didn't feel the weight of it all. Someone whispered the insults silently. The constant second-guessing. The emotional landmines she stepped on just by breathing too loud or asking the wrong question.

He controlled the money. She had to beg for things like milk or sanitary pads. He told her she didn't need a license, didn't need a job, didn't need friends. The fewer people around her, the better he could control the story. If she made a friend, he'd poison it—sow seeds of doubt, accuse her of gossiping, shame her into isolation.

Everything was her fault.

If the baby cried, she was spoiling him / her / it.
If the dinner wasn't hot enough, she was lazy.
If he was angry, she provoked it.
If he cheated, it was because she let herself go.
If he failed at something, it was because she distracted him with her incompetence.

He twisted every word, every situation, until she couldn't trust her own instincts. She started apologizing before speaking, saying, "I'm sorry" as a reflex. And that was exactly how he wanted it.

Gaslighting wasn't a word she knew. But she lived it every day.

When she cried, he called her dramatic.
When she doubted him, he said she was paranoid.
When she asked for kindness, he said she was
needy.
And when she finally screamed—just once—he
looked at her like *she* was the abuser.

He used silence as a weapon, too. Long stretches
where he wouldn't speak to her. Where he'd stomp
through the house, slam doors, make her feel like
she didn't exist until she broke down just to break
the tension. Then he'd act like she was "too
emotional." It was a cycle designed to keep her
begging for the very thing that hurt her.

She learned to walk on eggshells, to read his
moods like weather reports.
She became an expert in anticipating the next
storm.

And through it all, she still made dinner. She still
folded his clothes. Still rocked babies to sleep with
lullabies caught in her throat. She was a ghost in
her own life, haunting the kitchen, cleaning the
floor with a man's anger in every corner of the
room.

He would say, "You're lucky I stayed."
As if he were a gift.

As if staying in the cage he built was something we should all be grateful for.

But she didn't leave. Not because she didn't want to—but because she had nowhere to go. No education. No money. Four children who needed food, stability, survival. The system failed women like her.

So, she stayed.
And endured.

And we watched.

We saw her become smaller each year. She laughs less often now. Her back became more hunched. Her eyes grew dimmer. We knew something was wrong, but we didn't have the words for it. We just knew love wasn't supposed to feel like fear. Dads weren't supposed to make moms cry behind bathroom doors.

My mother never grew into the woman she could've been.

She was bright. Resourceful. Loving. But she lacked a nurturing. People used, cornered, and controlled her. Something prevented her from succeeding, but not her own shortcomings. And when she tried to rise, he was right there to clip her wings with a sharp word or an icy stare.

That's what emotional abuse is. It's not just yelling or name-calling.
It's a slow erosion of identity.
The stealing of confidence.
The deliberate shrinking of another human soul.

He never left bruises. But he left damage just the same.

And yet, she survived it.

She may have felt powerless, but she *wasn't*.
Even in all her pain, she still showed up.
Still mothered.
Still loved.
Still, she protected us to the best she could, even while no one protected her.

In the end, it wasn't her education that defined her.
It wasn't the eighth-grade diploma or the lack of credentials.
It was her heart.
Her grit.
Her ability to carry all of us—even while a man tried to convince her she was nothing.

But we knew better.

We saw her.
Even when he didn't.

Chapter 5

Oops, We Did It Again

Rejection...

Pregnancy should be a time of softness. Of anticipation. Of a woman folding her hands over her belly and imagining who her child might become. But in our house, pregnancy was another storm. Another reason for my father's rage to swell and crash into everything good.

My brother was the next storm.

We didn't know that phrase back then — "reproductive coercion." But that's exactly what it was. My mother didn't have an agency to go to for help. She didn't have power. She didn't even have a voice of her own body. By the time she was carrying her second child, she already knew how little choice she had in anything that involved her own life, much less her womb.

She was pregnant. Again.

And my father didn't want the baby. He didn't want the pregnancy. He didn't want *him.*

He acted as if it were her fault. As if she had deceived him. It seemed he wasn't as involved as if he hadn't known what he was doing. It was as though she had somehow *done this to him.*

He paced the floor. Snapped at everyone. Raged in whispers and glares, saving his worst behavior for behind closed doors. And then one night, he gave her something. A container. Given a command. A cruel, calculated demand:

Use this. You're not keeping that.

It was not medicine. The situation wasn't safe. It wasn't anything a doctor would ever prescribe.

It was acid.

He told her to douche with it—to kill the baby growing inside her. To flush it out as if it were something dirty. An inconvenience. A mistake.

My mother—exhausted, frightened, and already broken down from years of emotional abuse—did what he said.

She didn't want to.
She didn't believe it.
But something trapped her.

He trained her to obey. And when you live with a man like him, you stop asking "why" and start asking, "How do I survive this moment?" So, she did it. She used the acid. She followed his orders because the alternative felt even more terrifying.

She bled afterward.
Cramped.
Cried.

But the baby held on.

Somehow, against all odds, my brother survived. His tiny heart kept beating through the burn. Through the poison. Through the violence he didn't even know he was enduring.

And when he was finally born, my father didn't weep with joy. Instead, he kept a distance from him. He didn't even smile. He looked at him like a problem that hadn't gone away.

My brother was small. Fragile. But alive.

My mother held him with a mixture of awe and guilt. Before he ever took his first breath, she had tried to hurt him—no, someone had forced her to. He lived. To stay. To arrive anyway.

That's the thing about children born into chaos. They come out fighters. And my brother? He was a fighter from day one.

We joke now — "Oops, we did it again," like the world's saddest punchline to a pop song. But there was nothing lighthearted about it then. It was a phrase our father spat with bitterness. He didn't see his son as a blessing. He saw him as a mistake. A burden. Another mouth to feed, another responsibility he never wanted to carry.

He treated him like that for years.

And we all felt it.

My brother never got the soft voice, the gentle touch. He got the icy stare, the impatient sighs, the slammed doors. If crying too long meant he was "doing it on purpose."

He grew up in the shadow of not being wanted. And that shadow darkened everything.

My mother tried. She really did. She loved him fiercely. Held him tighter. Kissed him more often. But the guilt never left her. She knew what had almost happened. What someone had *done* to him before he even had a name.

She told him the truth when he was old enough to understand—not to wound him, but because lies rot the foundation of a person. And if there was one thing my mother believed in, it was that her children deserved the truth, even when it hurt.

He didn't cry when he heard it. He just stared at her for a long time. And then he said something she never forgot:

I already knew they did not want me.

But he wasn't bitter. Not like our father. Cruelty wasn't the reason he survived the pain. He turned it into something else. He turned it into strength. Into compassion. He promised never to emulate the man who had tried to erase him.

Sometimes when he laughs, I think about how close we came to never hearing that sound. How a few more seconds, a few more drops, and he wouldn't have made it. And I remember he is a walking miracle—not because he's perfect, but because he's *here*. Because he *shouldn't* be and *is not*.

He was never a mistake.
My father was.

He mistook control for love.
Power for parenting.
Obedience for respect.

But none of it could kill what survived.

My brother's life is proof of that. A testimony
written in laughter, scars, and stubborn,
unrelenting joy. Defiantly, he proclaimed with his
heartbeat, *"I will not be erased."*

"Oops, we did it again" wasn't just about another
baby. It was about hope breaking through cruelty.
About life choosing itself. About something good
growing in the ugliest soil.

And in that house of silence, pain, and poison—my
brother was the loudest declaration that love could
still win, even when it almost didn't.

Chapter 6

Trust Broken

Deceit...

Trust is supposed to be the foundation of a family. It's what children are born into without even knowing the word. It's what partners lean on when everything else feels unsteady. Trust is the invisible thread that ties people together through storms and silence. And once it's broken— especially again and again—it doesn't just disappear. It splinters. It infects everything.

In our house, trust didn't break in one big moment.

A thousand tiny breaks shattered it.

A look that didn't match the words. An unkept promise. A mood that changed without warning. It was that we never knew who we'd be dealing with when we walked through the door—whether he'd be charming or cruel, quiet, or explosive. It was the way he said "I love you" with a flat tone and then punished us for believing it.

But the first person who lost her trust, was my mom.

She was just a girl when she married him. Sixteen years old, pregnant, vulnerable, and already trained to put everyone else's needs before her own. She had no diploma, no career, and no support system. What she had was hope—and that's what he broke first.

He told her he'd love her. That he'd take care of her. That they'd raise a family together. But those words turned into shackles.

Her body, money, and choices were all controlled by him. So gradually he twisted love into fear, she did not realize what was happening until she didn't know how to leave. Fists weren't necessary for him. He employed shame. Silence was his weapon. He used emotional warfare so carefully, so consistently, that she doubted her own instincts.

She trusted him because she had been told to. Because the world said that a husband leads, and a wife follows. Because no one had ever taught her that genuine love doesn't make you smaller.

And we trusted her because she was our mother.

But as we got older, we saw it: the flinching, the constant apologies, the way her eyes scanned the room before she spoke—as if danger might hide behind every lamp. We didn't know the word for it then, but it was fear. And when children see fear in the one person who's supposed to protect them, something inside unravels.

We started questioning everything.

Was this normal?

Was this love?

Was this what dads were supposed to act?

He told us yes. That he was the provider. The protector. Everything he did was to "raise us right." But then he'd turn around and humiliate us, yell for no reason, tell us we were lucky he stayed.

He played mind games. Said one thing and did another. Apologized just enough to keep us off balance. Blamed us for our reactions. Made us doubt what we saw and felt. That's what emotional abuse does—it convinces you that you are the problem.

And we believed it.

We trusted him at first because we had no choice. He was our dad. He was the roof over our heads and the food on the table. But over time, we learned that nothing he gave came without a cost.

If he bought you something, you owed him gratitude forever.
If he let you go somewhere, he reminded you every time you messed up.
If you asked for help, he'd remind you that you were weak.

Trust became a trap.

And once we saw through it, we started guarding our hearts. No longer did we confide in him. We ceased bringing him problems. Honesty became dangerous, so we stopped being honest. Our honesty could betray us. He could twist it into lectures, punishments, or shame.

We learned to lie by omission. To fake smiles. To say "yes, sir" and "thank you" even when we were crumbling inside. That's what broken trust looks like in a child: obedience that smells like fear.

But it wasn't just us. He betrayed our mother's trust in ways we couldn't even see as kids. Affairs. Secrets. Half-truths slipped through the cracks of everyday life. He broke her spirit in whispers behind closed doors and long, empty silences at the dinner table.

He trained her not to ask questions. And when she did, he called her crazy.
That was the word he liked best—*crazy*.
He used it as a shield, like a sword.
If she cried, she was unstable.
If she pushed back, she was hysterical.
If she asked for more, she was selfish.

So, she stopped asking.

And that's what the erosion of trust really looks like. Not a dramatic explosion. Just the slow undoing of a person's voice. The turning down of the volume until all that's left is a whisper that says, *maybe this is all I deserve.*

But trust isn't just broken by betrayal. It's broken by inconsistency.

One day he'd take us for ice cream; the next he'd ignore us entirely. One day he'd say he was proud; Next, he'd call us disappointments. It was emotional whiplash. We were always on edge, waiting for the shift, the crack in the floor. It wasn't safe to believe anything was real.

Even the wonderful moments became suspicious.

If he was kind, we wondered what he wanted. If he was quiet, we braced for the storm. Trust wasn't trust—it was a countdown.

And the damage didn't stop when we left the house. It continued into our friendships, and our relationships. All of us carried it, we second-guessed compliments, we didn't believe in safety. We expected abandonment, manipulation, and betrayal.

Because we learned to love looks like that.

But here's the thing about broken trust: it doesn't have to be the end.

My mom—who had every reason to believe love was just another word for control—somehow kept her heart open. She loved us with a tenderness that was never shown to her. She tried in small, quiet ways to teach us that not everyone lies. Some people keep their promises. Genuine love doesn't hurt.

And over time, we healed.

Not all at once. Not completely. But we learned to spot the difference between fear and love. Between power and care. Between a voice that controls and a voice that comforts.

We still struggle sometimes. The ghost of broken trust doesn't leave easily. But we're not afraid to name them anymore. And that's how healing begins.

By telling the truth.

By recalling the items taken.
We reclaimed what we had lost.

Chapter 7

Baby #3

Unwelcomed...

By the time baby number three came along, the house was already full. Not with joy or chaos like in most growing families—but with tension, blame, and silence that wrapped around us like fog. Disgust, not wonder, greeted my mother's pregnancy announcement.

My father didn't want another child.

He didn't even pretend.

There was no soft hand on her belly. No talking of names or dreams. Just anger. Just disappointment. "You've ruined everything again," came the bitter words from cold eyes.

He didn't see her as a life, not a daughter. It's not a person. Not even a baby. He saw her as a mistake. A burden. Something to resent before she was even born.

My mother, still barely more than a child herself, carried that pregnancy with a heart full of fear and shame. She had two babies already, barely enough food, and a husband who reminded her daily that she was nothing more than a vessel for his unwanted consequences.

She put forth her best effort. That was her habit. She tried to smile. To hum lullabies while folding the tiny clothes someone had given her secondhand. But it was hard to celebrate when the man you share your bed with looks at your stomach like it's a betrayal.

And then baby number three arrived.

A beautiful little girl.

Perfect fingers. Soft curls. Eyes that searched for connection in a world that felt too cold for someone so small.

But my father didn't hold her.

Didn't rock her.
Didn't speak her name with pride.
He didn't want her, and he made sure we all knew it.

She cried a lot in the past weeks. And he'd say it was on purpose. That she was being "difficult." That she was trying to ruin his sleep. My mother, exhausted and alone in that house full of judgment, would try to soothe her, bouncing gently on her feet, whispering, "It's okay, baby, Mama loves you." But she was whispering it to herself, too. Because nothing felt okay.

Mom called her a blessing. She'd hold her close and say she was another chance-maybe her last one. But behind her eyes, we saw the fear. How would she protect this baby when she could barely protect herself.

We loved her. Fiercely. Because sometimes loving each other was all we had. And in that love, even if the world outside didn't notice, we made a promise-to never let her forget that she mattered. Because we knew there was no third wheel between us.

Chapter 8

Oh, Brother

Bond...

It wasn't a secret for long.

The whispers came first. Not from my father—he was never one to admit anything. But the whispers moved through the air like smoke. Thick. Slow. Inevitable. And when the truth finally surfaced, it cracked something open that had already been hanging on by threads.

My father had an affair.

Not his first. Probably not his last. But this one left behind something permanent—a child. The son. A boy born outside our home, outside our pain, outside the life we had built on silence and obedience. A boy who was everything we were not: wanted.

We didn't know him. We met him once—maybe twice. A blur in childhood memory. A quiet afternoon where our father made us sit still and be polite to a little boy we didn't understand. And then, like a ghost drifting in and out of a story, he was gone.

But we remembered our father's face.

His way: the way he lit up — when he was around him. The softening of his voice. The way he laughed—*laughed*—like something in him had opened. Like he was proud. Like this boy, this son from somewhere else, was the clean slate he always wanted. Unlike us. Not like the children born under obligation and control. Not like the children who lived in the house he resented.

That hurt in ways we couldn't put into words.

It wasn't just betrayal—it was replacement.

Here was this boy, born from someone else's arms, who got to experience a version of our father we never met. A father who smiled. Who played? Who showed up? Disappointment, shame, and bitterness toward our mother did not burden that father.

My mother took the news like a blade.

Previous events had humiliated her. She'd known his wandering eyes, his slippery words, the way he twisted things, so he was never wrong. But this was different. This was a baby. A living monument to her husband's disloyalty.

And worse—he was *happy* about it.

He didn't hide it. He didn't apologize. If anything, he wore it like a badge. Proof that he still had it. That someone else wanted him. That he could start again if he wanted to, without us. Without her. Without the life he pretended to suffer through.

We didn't talk about the boy after that.

He became a ghost on our family tree. No photos. No birthdays. No stories. Just a name whispered behind closed doors. My mother's face would harden if anyone mentioned him. And we—his children—learned to bury our curiosity under layers of hurt.

Because how do you ask about a brother who took your place in your own father's heart?

We wondered about him, though.

Did he know about us?

Did he know the father we had? The one who yelled more than he spoke, who controlled more than he cared, who withheld affection like it was a weapon?

51

Or did he see only the charming version? The one with the jokes and the crooked smile?

Did he grow up thinking he was lucky?

We knew better.

We knew what that man looked like when no one was watching. When the mask slipped. When the house was dark, the rage was real. We knew the damage he could do—not with fists, but with words sharp enough to bleed.

And maybe that's what hurt most.

That he saved the good parts of himself for someone else.

He could've been better. He had it in him. We saw it—for a moment—with that boy. We saw the potential. The tenderness he *chose* not to give us.

Make no mistake—it was a choice.

Warmth embraced him there, while coldness afflicted him here. He smiled at that boy and scowled at us. He loved with freedom once he'd already poisoned love in our home.

And for what?

A second chance?

A do-over?

He left emotional wreckage in his wake and then handed out sunshine like he hadn't taught us all how to live in shadow.

We never blamed the boy.

How could we? His birth was not a decision he made. He didn't ask to be caught in a web of secrets and infidelity and betrayal. He was just another child—just like us—dragged into a story written by someone else's cruelty.

But we felt the weight.

Of knowing we had a brother we couldn't talk about. A sibling we'd never know. A piece of our family tree grown in another garden. It made us feel smaller. Less worthy. Forgotten.

It reminded us that we were never enough for him.

This isn't his firstborn. Those infants resembling him were not. Not the toddlers who cried for him. Not the kids who waited for him to come home with softness in their eyes instead of anger on his breath.

He was in our past. His regret. His obligation.

But that boy? That boy was his prize.

Years later, someone asked if we'd ever met our half-brother. We said, "Yes, but we don't remember." And that's the truth. We met him, but we could not *see* him. Not as a brother. Not as family. Just as a reminder.

Of what we never got.

Of what he never gave.

Of what it meant to be born into a house full of punishment while someone else got the version of our father we begged for in silence.

Chapter 9

Behind the Curtain

Illusion...

If you looked at him from the outside, my father didn't seem like the type.

He wasn't movie-star handsome. He didn't walk into a room and make people stare. But he had something else—something quieter and more dangerous. A charm that worked like a trap. He knew how to make people feel seen, like they were the only ones in the room. Especially women. Especially when no one was watching.

The affairs started early—probably before the wedding ring was even warm on his finger. Maybe even while my mother was still carrying their first child, belly full of hope and heart full of belief that this man, this husband, would be her partner. Her protector.

Instead, he was a thief. He stole trust. Intimacy. Truth.

And he did it repeatedly.
Certain affairs extended for weeks. Some months.

Some, we suspect, even years. They happened in the shadows of grocery store aisles, at the corners of gas stations, in places that seemed ordinary until they were suddenly not. He had a way of making women feel needed, like he was a man misunderstood at home, a hero without a home front. He deliberately excluded his wife—my mother—from the performance he carefully staged.

She found out about them in pieces. Receipts in pockets. Perfume that wasn't hers. Late nights explained with thin lies. Whispers from neighbors. One woman even called the house once, asking for him by name. My mother picked up the phone. The silence on the other end said more than words ever could.

Still, she stayed.

Not because she didn't care. Not because she forgave. But what choice did she have? She had children. Lacking employment. No money. No high school diploma. She was stuck inside the marriage like a fly in amber, frozen in place while the world moved around her.

Every affair took a little more from her.

Her sense of pride. The sound of her voice. Her inability to trust her own reflection. She'd stand at the bathroom mirror some nights and ask questions no woman should have to ask: *Am I not enough? Am I ugly? Did I do something wrong?* And my father—if he ever heard those questions—would answer them with silence, or worse, with blame.

"You let yourself go."
"You're always nagging."
"You're just jealous."

He painted himself as the victim, and her as the jailer. As if cheating was something she forced him into. He acted as if he were a wild animal, incapable of being contained by vows, fatherhood, or the sight of her crying in the dark.

The cruelty of it wasn't just in the affairs—it was in the aftermath.

The way he'd act, it was like nothing happened. Like her heartbreak was an inconvenience. Like the pain she wore every day wasn't real. There were no apologies. No promises of change. Just a quiet agreement that things would keep going exactly as they had been.

And we—his children—saw more than he thought.

We felt the tension in the house. He slammed drawers. The long silences at dinner. We saw our mother shrinking, year by year, into someone more

57

ghost than woman. We watched our father disappear for hours, then he returned with that smug, calm demeanor that said, *"You can't touch me."*

And sometimes, we saw the women.

Once, my sister found a photograph in his glove box—a woman in lipstick and lace, smiling like she belonged there. Another time, I overheard a conversation in a parking lot. He didn't see me. But I saw him. Leaning too close. Smiling too wide. Making promises that didn't belong to him.

And then there was Beulah.

The one who came before everything. His fiancée. The one he was supposed to marry before my mother got pregnant and "ruined the plan." He never let go of her. Her name was a ghost in our home. He tucked her pictures away in drawers, slipped them into books, and hid them like relics. Not gone. Never gone. My mother had to live every day with the memory of the woman he *wanted*—while raising the children he *got*.

That wound never healed.

It just scabbed over and reopened again each time another woman appeared.

The lies became a rhythm. The shame is routine. My mother lived a double life—smiling for us, holding herself together in public, and crumbling in silence when the lights went out. She once told me, "I feel like I live in a house with all the windows open and nothing I say ever stays inside."

And he didn't care. He never cared.

For him, women were tools. Something to use, to enjoy, to discard. He wasn't in love with them—he was in love with the power. The chase. The feeling of being wanted, even if he had to destroy someone else to get it.

To him, he treated each new affair as just another act in a play he never stopped performing. Each woman thought she could change him. Each one learned the truth the hard way.

Behind the curtain, he was always the same man.

Unfaithful.
Unrepentant.
Unreachable.

And now, years later, the affair still echoes. Not just in memory, but in the way we love. In the way we flinch at kindness. In the way we question our worth. Because when you grow up watching someone betray the person who gave your life, it plants doubt in your bones. It teaches you that love can lie. People break promises.

But here's the truth:

My father was the broken one.
Not us.
Not my mother.
Not the women he used.
Not the children he disappointed.

He could love no one fully because he didn't even know how to love himself without a mirror reflecting admiration back at him.

We may have been born into the wreckage, but we're the ones who climbed out of it. We're the ones who found loyalty in places he never looked. Who stitched trust back together, one hard-earned thread at a time.

Behind the curtain, he was nothing but smoke and shadow.
But we—his children—became the light.

Chapter 10

Eleven Months

Refuge...

They used to say I took eleven months to be born.

Of course, that's impossible. No pregnancy lasts that long. No doctor would allow it; nobody could hold on for nearly a year. But in my family, it became a kind of legend—whispered with half a laugh and half a sadness that no one ever named.

"Eleven months," my mom would say, her eyes far off, her voice gentle. "You just didn't want to come out."

And I believe it.

Because something in me must have known.

The world waiting for me wasn't soft. It wasn't the place a baby should rush into. I imagine myself curled up tight in her womb, hands against my ears, trying to block out the shouting, the silence, the weight pressing against us both.

Maybe I knew what was waiting on the other side of breath.
Maybe I already felt the fear in her heartbeat.

She was incredibly young. So tired. So broken down already by life and marriage and all the things a girl shouldn't have to carry before she's even old enough to vote. I was her fourth child. Her third daughter. Her baby and her last chance to get something right.

She'd rub her belly and talk to me when no one was around. Whisper secrets through skin. Cry quietly into her pillow, apologizing for things I hadn't even lived yet.

And I stayed. Eleven months, she said. Well past the due date. Long after the doctors gave worried looks. Long after no one could explain why I hadn't come yet. But I knew why.

Because the womb was the only place I was safe.

There, the air was warm. The rhythm of her heartbeat was steady, even when her real life was not. No slammed doors. I got to avoid harsh language. No glances that cut. Just the deep, quiet hum of survival.

I stayed because I was listening.
I could hear the way her voice cracked when he

came home.
I felt the way her body tensed when he walked by.
Even unborn, I understood fear.

And outside that womb was a man who didn't
want me.

Not because he knew me. Not because I had done
anything wrong. But because I was another
responsibility. Another mouth to feed. Another
reminder that control was slipping through his
fingers. I was born into resentment I hadn't earned.
Into a house that would never feel like home.

Maybe that's why I took my time.

Maybe that's why labor came like a whisper
instead of a scream. My mother says I was born
small. Quiet, wide-eyed. Like I had already seen
too much. Him not holding me did not surprise me.

She gave birth to me at St. Mary's in Lima, Ohio.
"It's was a gray day," she said. Not cold, not
warm. Just in-between. She labored in silence,
gripping the rails of the hospital bed, gritting her
teeth through the pain. No one rubbed her back.
No one coached her through the contractions. She
was alone, even when the room wasn't empty.

And then I came.

Not screaming. Not kicking. Just there.

Like I had finally given up on hiding.

She held me to her chest and cried—not from joy, but from everything else. From the fear that it would all happen again. Because of the added strain of another child on an already strained household. I feel guilty for not being able to protect myself from him.

But she loved me. God, did she love me.

She told me that part too. Even when exhausted and heartbroken, my presence soothed her. That holding me reminded her of softness. That maybe—just maybe—I could grow into something stronger than the shadows I was born into.

She would say, "You were stubborn from the beginning. Eleven months in there, like you knew better."

And maybe I did.

Perhaps the house to which they brought me was full of noise and secrets. Maybe I sensed the chaos. Maybe I already understood that this life— *my* life—was going to be one long climb out of the rubble.

I've carried that story with me for as long as I can remember.

"Eleven months." It's funny and sad all at once. A family joke with roots in something darker. A myth built for survival. But also, a truth too deep for science to explain. A soul's truth. A knowing.

Because some babies leap into the world.

And others linger.

Waiting.
Listening.
Bracing.

Even now, as an adult, I hesitate sometimes. Taking too long to decide. Overthinking. Sitting in the dark a few minutes longer than I need to. I wonder if part of me is still curled up in that space, waiting for a sign that it's safe to come out.

But eventually, I do.

I always do.

Because the world is hard, yes—but it's also full of light I never expected. People who do not cause harm. Of places where doors don't slam. Of mornings that don't start in fear.

My mom was right. I wanted to stay in.
But I came out anyway.

And every step I've taken since has been an act of defiance. A refusal to let fear be the entire story. A promise to the baby I once was: *You made it. Now live.*

So, I do.

I live for the eleven-month-old newborn. Though born without crying, she already understood the meaning of tears. Dedicated to the daughter of a woman who loved her despite everything. For the life that tried to delay itself until it could find a softer world.

And maybe, one day, I'll tell my story to someone else—someone small, someone listening.

And I'll say:

"You took your time. But that's okay. Some souls are too sensitive for this world and need a little more time before they face it. I know. I was one of them

Chapter 11

Bless the Beasts and the Children

Innocence...

Bless the beasts and the children, for in this world they have no voice. They have no choice.

That line echoed in my head more times than I can count. I didn't hear it first in church or in a book. I heard it on the radio, in the background of life, during long car rides through small towns and louder silences. But it stayed with me because even as a child, I knew what it meant.

Because we were children.

And we lived among the beasts.

Not monsters in the traditional sense. Not claws and teeth and red eyes in the dark. But beasts that wore human skin. Beasts that sat at the dinner table and paid the electric bill and tucked you in at night with hands that had just finished tearing down your mother's soul.

The beasts were people no one warned you about.

Charm endowed them. Holding each other, they embraced. They had legal names and voter registrations. They shook hands at church and knew how to make casseroles. But behind closed doors, their roars came as slammed doors and slow, cutting words. And children, like us, absorbed those sounds into their skin.

We learned to recognize the storms before they arrived.

The alteration in footstep rhythm. Our mother's smile held a stiffness. The way the air got heavier just before the yelling started. That was our barometer. Our survival skill. Our childhood.

And bless the children indeed.

Because we didn't ask for any of it. Broken promises are not what I want. Not the confusion. Not the homes filled with rage instead of warmth. We didn't choose to be born into a war we couldn't name, where the enemy was the man in the recliner, and silence was our only defense.

We were children who made excuses for bruises that didn't show.

Children who flinched at kindness because they didn't trust it. Who believed that love came with strings attached and that affection was a tool used

to control. We were too young to know the word
"manipulation," but we knew how it felt.

We were hungry—not just for food, though
sometimes that too—but for peace. For softness.
For a love that doesn't change form when it comes
inside.

And still—we kept going.

There was a game we played. Occasionally, we
laughed. We found magic in dandelions and in
moments under the covers with a flashlight and a
book. We survived because children always
survive. But survival isn't living. And in those
quiet corners of our hearts, we carried scars we
couldn't name.

And what about the beasts?

Bless them, too?

That's harder to say. Because the beast in our
house was our father. And no matter how many
times he hurt us—emotionally, psychologically,
with silence more than fists—he was still the one
whose blood ran through our veins.

But if you trace his story back far enough, there's
sorrow there too.

He never healed.

And unhealed boys grow into wounded beasts.

That doesn't excuse what he did. Not to us. Not to my mother. But it explains why he turned into someone who couldn't love the way we needed. He was still responsible for the pain he caused— but maybe, just maybe, the beast deserved something too: understanding. Not forgiveness. Not freedom. But the acknowledgment that even monsters have origin stories.

Bless the beasts and the children.

Both are casualties of something bigger.

Systemic silence. Generational trauma. A world that doesn't know how to hold broken people without dropping them again. The beasts lash out because they don't know how to be held. The weight of the world crushes children because they shouldn't carry so much.

We carried more than backpacks.

We carried our mothers' sorrow. Our fathers' rage. The unspoken rules of survival. We carried the burden of pretending everything was fine when nothing was. We went to school. Still, we made friends. Still, we dreamed. That's the miracle of children. Their resilience.

But it comes at a cost.

It catches up eventually.

Chapter 12

Nightmare on Vine Street

Terror...

I was two years old.

Too young to understand fear, but old enough to feel it settle in my bones. Old enough to sense the shift in the air before things exploded. Old enough to recognize the darkness in a man's eyes—even if that man was my father.

Vine Street sounds harmless, like a place where porches sag under the weight of flowerpots and children play hopscotch in chalked-out squares. But for me, Vine Street is where innocence ended. It's where the world stopped being safe. I learned far too early that monsters don't always hide in closets. Sometimes, they wear your last name.

That night, my father snapped.

There was no buildup, no warning. Just a flash of something violent and unpredictable. My siblings cried. Someone grabbed me—a toddler. Lifted. Dragged into the kitchen like a rag doll.

And then the knife.
Cold pressed against the soft skin of my throat.

He was going to kill me.

It's a correct statement. That's not an exaggeration. That's the truth. My father held a blade to my neck with every intention of ending my life. His own child. His baby. He might have seen it to exert control. Maybe he saw it as punishment. Maybe he wasn't seeing anything at all—just red, just rage, just the crumbling fragments of a man losing his grip on reality.

I don't remember the knife. Not the metal. Not the pressure. But trauma has a way of branding itself onto your body, even when your mind is too young to hold the memory. I carry that night inside me like a scar only I can feel. And I carry the silence that followed it, too.

The police came. Someone called them—maybe a neighbor, maybe my mother, maybe God himself. They pulled him off me. They arrested him. And for once, he didn't charm his way out. It was impossible to smooth this over. Not this time.

They sent him to a mental institution. Locked away. Labeled. But labels don't heal wounds. And locked doors don't undo what's already been done. My father left the house in handcuffs, but the damage stayed behind. Within the walls. In the air. A death sentence barely missed the little girl.

And then came the silence.

No one wanted to talk about it. The ones who are not the neighbors. Not the church folk. Not our family. The situation left us alone and my mother needed answers. She had forced herself to suppress her grief with the realization that she had married a man she thought she could endure, but how do you endure someone who nearly kills your children?

She tried to keep us together. Tried to find help. Tried to reach out to the people who should have stepped up.

However, numerous individuals declined.

They didn't take us in. Didn't say, *come stay here. Let us help.* Its possible fear was the reason. Maybe they were ashamed. Maybe they didn't want to look too closely at what this man had become. Perhaps they could not love children with shattered lives.
Our abandonment forced us to fend for ourselves. They shuffled us. Strained. Fractured.

I don't remember being held after that night. I don't remember anyone telling me I was safe. And that's the saddest part—when you're two years old and no one tells you it's going to be okay, you grow up believing it never will be.

People ask how someone so young can carry trauma.

To them, I conveyed my uncertainty about the knife, but my certainty that the room had changed. I knew the air was wrong. I knew the eyes looking down at me didn't see me as a daughter anymore—but as something to destroy. You mustn't forget that, even if your memory can't frame it in words.

And the aftermath? It was quieter. But no less cruel.

We learned to survive without asking for comfort. We learned that crying didn't bring anyone running. That fear had to be swallowed, tucked into tiny bodies that had already seen too much. I watched my siblings grow guarded. I watched my mother wear strength like armor that didn't quite fit. And I—just a toddler—learned to watch everyone else, to gauge danger in the smallest shifts.

Our house was still on Vine Street, but it was never a home again. The shadows got longer. The rooms got colder. There was no lullaby that could undo what had almost happened in that kitchen.

I should not have lived.
But I did.

And for a long time, that survival felt like a burden. Like I had to justify it. Prove I was worth the second chance. But now I see it for what it is: a defiance. A refusal to be erased. A heartbeat that said, *not today. Not this time.*

I grew up. He got out. We all carried it differently.

But Vine Street never left us.

It's not just a memory. It's a turning point. The moment everything shifted, the night our family stopped pretending. Someone ripped the curtain wide open. And in its place was the truth: that evil can wear a smile, that danger can grow inside your own walls, and that violence can mark even the smallest child.

I was two years old.
And I lived.
Not untouched. Not unscathed.
But *alive.*

And now, every word I write is another inch away from that knife.

Every truth I speak is one more stitch in the wound.

He tried to end me.
But I'm still here.

Chapter 13

The Phone Call

Snap...

It started with a ring.

Only: It's just a phone call. Just a question. Just a man trying to reach his wife in a small hospital in Ohio. But that one call shattered the core of our family, unleashing something dark—something we could never repair.

My mother had gone to the hospital for a procedure. That's what she told him. Something simple. Something routine. She didn't give details, and he didn't ask. They weren't in love anymore. Maybe they never were. But even through the distance and resentment, he still picked up the phone to check in. Perhaps it was out of habit. Maybe out of suspicion. Maybe both.

He called the hospital. Gave her full name. Told the nurse he was her husband and asked how she was doing.

And that's when it happened.

A pause on the other end of the line. A shuffle of papers. Then a voice, too casual, too careless, spoke words that set everything on fire.

"Oh yes," the nurse said, "she's the one here for the abortion."

Silence.

My father didn't respond immediately. His body went still, fingers frozen around the receiver. Blood drained from his face. His mouth opened, but no sound came out. Something in him broke right there, in that space between what he thought was true and what he'd just heard.

She was having an abortion.

But how?
He'd had a vasectomy.

The math didn't add up, and his mind couldn't handle the equation. Betrayal. Confusion. Rage. They collided in an instant, blinding him with the force of it.

He hung up without another word.

What came next wasn't a measured response. It wasn't anger laced with sadness or grief tinged

with reason. It was something else entirely—
something primal. Something fractured.

He snapped.

That's what they called it later. Taking a break. A
psychotic episode. A sudden descent into
something unrecognizable. But for those of us who
lived it, it didn't feel sudden at all. It felt like the
final domino, toppled after years of tension and
cruelty and quiet madness.

He showed up at the hospital. Screaming.
Demanding. Unraveling causing the nurses to back
away.

By then, he had severed whatever tether that had
kept him connected to our world.

They diagnosed him with schizophrenia.

It made sense in hindsight. Paranoia can be
overwhelming. The delusions. The way he twisted
conversations, rewrote memories, made everyone
feel like they were walking through fog. He had
always danced on the edge of something
dangerous. Now, there was a name for it.

But a diagnosis didn't fix what he'd done. It didn't
erase the fear or the trauma, or the legacy of
damage he'd carved into each of us like initials in

wet cement. And it didn't bring back the pieces of my mother that had shattered long before that phone call.

She had carried his children. Cooked his meals. Survived his cruelty. And yet he still believed she'd betrayed him. That one nurse's mistake— one slip of the tongue—was all it took to tip him over.

The truth?

She wasn't having an abortion.

The nurse had confused her with another patient. My mother had come in for something entirely different. But the damage was already done. The words had burrowed deep. And for a man like my father, words were never just words. They were weapons. Triggers. Proof of the war he always believed the world was waging against him.

After his institutionalization, people tried to explain it all away. Mental illness. Tragedy. Misunderstanding. But we knew better. We knew that the illness wasn't the entire story. Before the diagnosis, cruelty had already begun. Manipulation is happening. The control. The way he made us question reality even before his own slipped.

And I can't stop thinking about that nurse.
Did she ever find out what her mistake caused?
Did she go home that night and eat dinner like it
was any other shift?
Or did someone tell her she had broken up a family
with her misstatement?

We'll never know.

What I know is this: that call was a turning point.
Before it, things were tense. Damaged. Cracked.
But after it, the call shattered us. My mother never
looked at phones the same way again. For years,
she'd flinch when one rang. My siblings and I
learned that a single sentence could destroy
everything. That misunderstanding could be as
dangerous as malice.

And my father—well, he was never truly the same.
Maybe he had never been.

He faded into the system, into diagnoses and
medications and supervised visits that never came.
Eventually, he became a ghost we rarely spoke of,
except in cautious tones and late-night whispers.

But I remember the day it changed.
The day of the call.
The day one sentence became a storm.
The day we all stopped pretending we were a

family and accepted we were survivors of one man's unraveling.

Just a phone call.

But everything after it was different.

Chapter 14

Split Apart

Scattered...

After they pulled away the knife and finally took my father out of the house, we thought maybe—just maybe—the worst was over.

We were wrong.

Sometimes the aftermath of violence leaves a deeper scar than the violence itself. After locking him away, they lacked a plan. No soft landing. No emergency net stretched out to catch us. There were just four children, stunned and silent, looking up at adults who didn't know what to do with broken pieces.

And so, they split us apart.

Relatives took my two sisters in—distant branches of the family tree we barely knew. There was no long goodbye. No chance to hold each other one last time. Just a car door shutting and the sound of people telling us we'd be "better off this way."

Better off.

I hate those words. They always seem to be used when something is being taken from you.

They left my brother and me. The other two and me being the youngest. The ones too small, too complicated, too inconvenient to place with anyone we knew. Our grandparents said no. Other family closed their doors. Maybe they were afraid of what we'd bring with us—too much history, too many questions, too much pain.

So, the state stepped in.

They took my brother one way, and me another. No one asked if we wanted to stay together. No one asked anything at all. We were paperwork. Case files. Checklists. And just like that, they tore away the last thread of safety—our bond as siblings.

A foster family took me in. And by some twist of fate, they were kind. I don't know how long I stayed—maybe a year, maybe less—but I remember the swing set in their backyard. It had blue seats and long chains, and when I closed my eyes and tilted my head to the sky, I felt something I hadn't in a long time: lightness.

The mother smelled of vanilla. She knelt when she talked to me, like I mattered. With gentle hands, the father called me "kiddo." They didn't push.

They just let me *be*. For a child who came from chaos, even small kindness felt like a miracle. Unbeknownst to me, that moment of peace would remain with me for life, a cosmic whisper seeming to say, *"See?" It doesn't always have to hurt.*

But while I was swinging in sunlight, my brother was living in the dark.

They put him in an orphanage. It was a cold, hard place where rows of beds stood, and love had long since disappeared. They didn't just forget him there—they broke him. Hurt by hands that were supposed to care for him. Abused by those who called themselves guardians. He told me later that it felt like a prison for children. The only thing that changed was the jailer's name.

He stayed as long as he could bear. Then, one day, he ran.

No shoes. No food. Just instinct and fear and the desperate need to escape. He ran through back alleys and across schoolyards. He hid behind dumpsters. He was hungry. But he was free. And in that freedom, he stumbled upon something rare: a sliver of compassion.

A police officer found him.

Not a social worker. Not the system. A Police officer. Someone who noticed the bruises, the hunger, the silence that spoke louder than any scream. He didn't just report him—he *took him in.* Gave him a place to sleep. Fed him. Looked him in the eyes, like he was a person worth saving.

He didn't have to.
But he did.

And maybe that's what saved him.

We wouldn't reunite for some time. The wind scattered us like leaves. But we survived. Somehow, we kept breathing. Kept going. Even when the world seemed determined to forget we ever existed.

Years later, when I asked about those days, my brother told me the police officer, and his wife never asked him what he had done—only what he needed. That one question changed everything.

It's strange how memories fracture. I don't remember the car ride that took me away. I don't remember what I was wearing or what I said. But I remember that swing set. I remember my brother's eyes the last time I saw him before they pulled us apart — wide and confused, holding back tears like a boy already learning that crying got you nowhere.

I remember the silence in the car.
And the quiet ache of knowing we were no longer
"we."

We were no longer a family.
Just fragments.

Split apart.

Chapter 15

David and Goliath

Resilience...

When they took my brother from me, it felt like someone ripped half my heart out and didn't bother stitching up the wound.

I was too little to understand why we couldn't stay together. I just knew that suddenly he was gone. One moment we were side by side, surviving together in a home that didn't know how to love us—and the next, I was alone in a strange house with strangers calling themselves family, and he was somewhere else entirely.

I thought of him constantly.

At night, I'd look out the window and imagine him under the same sky, wondering where I was. I'd picture him brave, strong like David from the Bible stories—facing his own Goliaths, refusing to back down. I told myself he was okay, that someone kind was watching over him. That wherever he was, he was safe. Perhaps he owned a dog. Maybe he had a room with a nightlight.

Maybe he got to eat warm pancakes and sit on someone's lap during thunderstorms.

Those thoughts were all I had.
They were how I survived the ache.

But when I got older and found out the truth, my heart sank.

He hadn't been with a kind family. He'd been in an orphanage. Cold. Isolated. Forgotten. And not only had they failed to protect him—they'd hurt him. Again, and again. People who were supposed to care became the new monsters. He had run away just to save himself. A child running from the very place that should have saved him.

And all that time, I had imagined him smiling.

I think a part of me broke when I learned what he'd been through. It was grief layered on top of guilt—because while I'd been swinging on a backyard swing set, trying to pretend life was soft and safe, he'd been living in the darkness no child should ever know.

We were just kids.
But different storms challenged us.
Something forced us to do it alone.

Then, one day, everything changed.

I still remember it like a dream. The retail complex. The noise was loud. In the distance a spinning carousel with lights. And the Ferris wheel—bright, colorful, rising above the food court like some minor miracle. That's where we found each other again. They built a machine with arms to lift people high enough for a view of everything.

We reunited.

My mother, my brother, my sisters, and me. Each of us standing there a year older, battle-worn, but breathing. Whole in body, if not in spirit. I don't remember who hugged whom first. I just remember the way time froze for a second. The way the noise of the mall faded, and all I could hear was the sound of my heart pounding against ribs that had carried so much.

We had made it back to each other.

We didn't go home that day. Not to the homes we had come from. Forward we went. We moved to Ada, Ohio—a tiny farm town that smelled like hay and felt like distance. We lived on a small farm where the days were long; The work was hard, and the nights came heavy and quiet. But there was space there. There was land. There were animals.

And for the first time, it felt like maybe we could breathe.

My mother tried to hold us together. She really did. But life had stripped her of too much, too soon. She had grown up poor, dropped out early, married young. Life had beaten her down, and by a man who used love as a leash. And though she had left him—though she had *tried*—there were strings tied to us she couldn't cut.

She told us that if she divorced him, she'd lose us. That the courts would take us from her. That he'd win.

So, she went back.

Not because she wanted him. But because she couldn't stand to lose us. She chose survival over freedom. Her love for us was bigger than her hatred of him. And that is its own kind of heartbreak—watching someone walk back into a cage to keep the door open for the people they love.

Back then, I lacked understanding. My youth prevented me from understanding the gravity of her decision. I knew only that the man who once held a knife to my throat was back under the same roof. I knew only that my brother, who had finally

come back into my world, might now see all of it
unravel again.

But we stayed.
In Ada
On the farm.
Together.

Effectively, we used our resources.

When he was angry, we learned to move quietly
and disappear as the tension rose. We clung to
each other like shipwreck survivors. Because we
were. Each of us had his or her own story. Our
own nightmare. But now, we were on the same
chapter again.

I've always thought of my brother as David. Small
but mighty. A boy who stood up against monsters
bigger than himself and survived. But now I see
we were both David. Both facing Goliaths no child
should ever face. The system. Violence is present.
Following the split. The lies. The silence.

And somehow, we made it.

Not without scars. Not without pain. But with a
kind of strength that still hums beneath our skin.
Something tore us apart.
Someone put us through hell.

And we found our way back—under the blinking
lights of a Ferris wheel in a noisy mall.

Where once there was silence, now there was
laughter.
Where once there was distance, now there was
home.

And we held on to each other.
Like David would've done.

Chapter 16

The Farm Years

Pause...

Life on the farm, Ohio, wasn't easy. But it was ours.

It was the first place we landed after the chaos. A dusty old rental with warped floorboards, broken fencing, and a barn that leaned like it had secrets. But there was land, and for a while, there was laughter. Although we still carried the bruises from the past, we found freedom in those fields.

And trouble.

One morning, when the snow had fallen thick, I knew on the store counter there was a cookie shaped like a smiley face. It was perfectly round, yellow-frosted and it had my name on it. I knew my mom was at the store across the wheat field and I only three at the time and barely old enough to understand restraint—and the cookie was calling my name.

I didn't bother with shoes. Or socks. Or clothes.

I ran—*naked*—through the snow, straight across the frozen yard, chasing that cookie like it was gold. My feet turned red, then blue. The wind sliced my skin like tiny knives. But I didn't care. The cold didn't matter. I wanted the cookie. It was probably the only sweet thing in the store.

I entered the store, and the owner inquired of my mother, "Is that your child?" I took a bite and smiled.

Then I heard my siblings laughing behind me, doubled over in the store doorway as they saw me—wild-haired, shivering, with crumbs on my lips and snow on my bare legs. That cookie may have lasted five minutes. But the story? It's lasted a lifetime.

We survived on that farm. Sometimes in silence. Sometimes in screaming.

It was like the day my brother burned down the wheatfield.

It began with a match. He had seen adults' light bonfires and wanted to try it himself. Though he meant no harm, curiosity and dry stalks are a dangerous combination.

Flames roared to life. Orange. Crackling.
Terrifying.

We stood frozen as the fire chewed its way
through the dry wheat, faster than we could
scream. Our mom came running with a wet towel
and a bucket, screaming louder than the fire,
swearing through the smoke. The fire scorched the
field's edge before we put it out—but the smell
lingered for weeks. So did the fear in my brother's
eyes.

Jail was what he thought he was facing. He
thought the police would come. He didn't sleep for
days. And yet, we never stopped playing. Because
that's what kids do. Even in the ashes, we climb.

We found the best escape at the top of the barn.

There was a wooden beam across the rafters, and if
you were brave enough to climb it, there hung a
thick old rope. We'd grab it, hearts pounding, and
swing out over the loft—screaming, flying,
weightless—and then let go, landing with a thud
into the hay pile below.

The hay smelled of summer and dust. It scratched
our arms, filled our hair with bits of straw, and left
us giggling. For a moment, we were pirates.
Acrobats. Superheroes. No trauma. No past. Just
flight.

But even freedom has a time limit.

The day the landlord came, everything stopped.

He pulled into the driveway in a rusted truck, boots crunching on gravel. His voice was bitter, matter of fact. "You've got to go," he said. Just like that. No kindness. No notice. Get to the point. The rent remained unpaid. He was selling. We were out.

Mom didn't fight. She didn't scream. She just nodded, lips pressed tight, her eyes going glassy. We had nowhere to go. Again.

We packed in silence. Toys, hand-me-downs. Blankets that smelled like wood smoke. The swing set we had begged for stayed behind. So did the rope in the barn. So did our laughter.

And then we left.

We didn't just move houses—we moved *lives*. Left everything, we knew. Friends. School. The fields that held our footsteps. The farmhouse that echoed with our noise. And we headed south.

I remember the road stretching in front of us like a question we couldn't answer. No map. No certainty. Just a car full of kids and a mother holding on with fingers that had forgotten what it felt like to rest.

We left not because we wanted to but because my dad filed bankruptcy and he was embarrassed to stay in Ohio.

We followed. Like baby birds trailing behind a mother too broken to fly, but too brave not to try.

The farm years were over.
The snow.
The swing.
The fire.
The freedom.

But we carried them with us.

Even in chaos, there had been moments of magic. Even in poverty, there had been wonder. And even as children of trauma, we had lived, to laugh, to love—if only for a little while.

We had run through snow.
We had swung from the rafters.
We had touched the sky.

And no one could take that from us.

Chapter 17

The Lake

Desperation...

We were supposed to be going to Arizona.

That's what they said. That's where the sun lived, where things were going to be better, where maybe we'd finally land for good. I didn't know what Arizona was. I thought maybe it had castles, or sand you could eat, or beds made of clouds. But we never got there.

We got stuck in Texas.
And then we ended up at the lake.

Benbrook Lake. The name sounded nice enough. Like a place where ducks swam, and kids splashed, and grown-ups laughed while cooking hot dogs. But for us, it wasn't a vacation. It was survival. And for me—just four years old—it was terrifying.

We lived in a tent. Not the cozy kind. Not the kind you see in cartoons with zippers and stars overhead. Ours was old and smelled like mildew and wet socks. It flapped in the wind and leaked when it rained. There were nights the wind was so loud it sounded like monsters crawling across the canvas. I'd bury my head under a blanket and pretend it was a shield.

At four, your imagination fills in the gaps. When adults don't explain, your mind does the work. And my mind saw shadows. My vision: In the woods, I pictured creatures with yellow eyes and long claws, waiting for little kids who wandered too far. I feared the lake would swallow me whole. I believed the coyotes I sometimes heard at night were ghosts of children who never made it out.

I didn't understand the meaning of "homeless," but I felt scared.

There were no bathrooms. We went into the woods. My mom would take my hand and lead me into the brush and tell me to watch out for thorns and snakes. I thought maybe a snake would rise like a rope and wrap around my leg, pulling me into the dirt. So, I learned to pad. To stay close. To listen for rustling leaves as if it meant something was coming.

We had little food. I remember crackers. Sometimes beans come in a can. Once, someone gave us a loaf of bread, and we all treated it like cake. We sat around and ate it as if it were Christmas dinner. I thought maybe if I didn't eat too much, there'd be enough for tomorrow. But tomorrow always came hungry.

My clothes were dirty. I didn't mind so much—until I noticed other kids didn't look like me. Sometimes families would camp nearby with shiny campers and clean shoes. They'd ride bikes and laugh and roast marshmallows. I watched from a distance, hiding behind a tree, feeling like I was something other than a child. Like I didn't belong in their world of campfires and bedtime stories.

At night, it got colder than I thought Texas should be. My mom would wrap me in blankets that didn't match, whisper stories I only half-understood, and promise me we'd be okay. But even at four, I could hear the tired in her voice. The worry in her eyes. She was trying to be brave for us. And we were trying not to let her know how scared we were.

One night, I woke up to shouting. Loud voices. A truck. A flashlight cut through the trees like a blade. I thought someone had taken us away. My heartbeat was so loud I thought it would wake up the forest. My brother held my hand. I think I squeezed his until his fingers went numb. The men left eventually, but after that, I never really slept at the lake again. Just rested with one eye open.

We bathed in the lake. Chilly water. It made my teeth chatter. Mom would dip a rag in and scrub our faces, our arms. Sometimes she'd hum while she did it, trying to make it feel like a game. But it never felt like a game. It felt like we were trying to wash something off that didn't come from dirt.

I started making up stories in my head. About why we were there. I told myself we were hiding from dragons. That our tent was a secret fort. That we were special warriors waiting for a sign to tell us what to do next. It was easier than the truth. Easier than facing the way people looked at us when we walked into a gas station with coins instead of dollars.

One day, someone told us to leave.

We finished camping. No more space. No more pretending we were invisible. Whether it was a park ranger, or a police officer is unclear to me. When my mom was folding the tent, I remembered, she did so with a curious blend of affection and animosity. I remember throwing out my only pair of shoes because they were wet and moldy. I remember her saying, "We're leaving the lake," and I didn't know whether to feel relief or more fear.

We never made it to Arizona.

But we left the lake behind us.
The frosty nights.
The fear.
The creatures in the woods my four-year-old mind
believed were real.

Sometimes I think about that lake.
About how it swallowed part of my childhood.
About how it taught me that being poor doesn't
just mean no money—it means no safety. No
home. No certainty.

But it also taught me something else:
Even in the scariest places, children imagine light.
And even in the deepest dark, we dream.

Chapter 18

Back in the Fire

Relapse...

We should never have moved to Michael Street.
Even our friends told us not to.

They'd heard stories. Whispers. Warnings. That
street had a name that didn't just carry mail—it
carried memories, scars, danger. People said the
neighborhood wasn't safe. People said a curse
afflicted the house. Said nothing good ever lasted
there.

But none of it mattered to my father.

He decided, like he always did—alone, without
care or concern for what we wanted or what we
feared. He said it was cheap. Said it was a "fresh
start." But deep down, we knew this wasn't a
beginning. It was a return. A reopening of wounds
we'd just barely stitched shut.

He signed the lease. Packed the car.
And we went.
Back into the fire.

Instantly the moment we arrived, the feeling hit me. Looming over us, the house seemed to know we were coming. The porch sagged like a tired mouth, the paint peeling like skin. The windows were clouded, as if they didn't want to see what would happen inside them. It wasn't a home—it was a warning.

But we didn't get to say no.

I wanted to scream. To beg my mother not to go inside. But I saw the look in her eyes. That familiar mix of resignation and quiet terror. That was beneath her dignity. She'd been fighting fires for years, and this time, she didn't have the strength to put up the hose. She walked in with the rest of us—head down, voice gone.

And just like that, we were back.

Back in the same pattern. Fear remains constant. The same clenched fists, not always raised, but always felt. The same walls that listened to every whisper, every threat, every lie. It didn't take long. We unpacked boxes with our hands and dread in our hearts.

The neighbors watched. Some from behind curtains. Some were bold enough to step onto porches and call out, "You know who used to live there, right?" Like maybe we didn't already feel the weight of it. One woman pulled my mom aside and said, "You shouldn't have come here. That house eats people."

She wasn't wrong.

At Michael Street, we were ghosts in training. You learn to walk without a sound. Breathe without being noticed. Speak in apologies. Sleep with one eye open. We'd lived through chaos before, but this house was something else. It had a memory. It remembered pain. And it welcomed more.

The heat in the summer made the air thick with sweat and silence. The winter cracked the glass in the windows and left ice inside. But it was the nights that burned most. Because at night, my father came alive. The rage. After experiencing the bitterness. The endless need to remind us we were his *property*.

He'd slam cabinets. Accuse. Pace the halls like a warden. We never knew what would set him off. We could hear a sound. A look. Someone found a sock on the floor. Everything matched. And it was full of gasoline.

My brother tried to stay quiet, but you could see it in the way his jaw clenched—that same fire beginning to grow inside him. My sisters clung to each other, pretending their shared bed was a fortress. And me? Unassuming, I remained. I became invisible. I became what every child in a house like that must become: a shadow with a heartbeat.

There were wonderful moments. Laughter, we stole when he wasn't looking. Stories whispered under covers. The time my brother found a kitten in the alley and snuck it inside for a day. The way my mom hummed when she brushed my hair, even if her hands were shaking.

But mostly, it was survival.
Again.
Still.

Friends stopped coming over. They didn't want to be near the house. Some said their parents forbade it. Others just stopped talking to us. We couldn't blame them. We were radioactive. Burned too many times to pretend we were normal.

Every day at the house felt like walking barefoot across coals.

And yet, my father called it "home."
As if it were something warm.
As if the fire didn't burn his children every time he opened his mouth.

He said we should be grateful. That we had a roof. That we had him. He told us over and over, "No one else would take you." And after a while, some parts of us believed it. Because when all you've ever known is fire, you think the smoke is air.

Deep inside, I knew this wasn't right. I knew someone had warned us.
And we hadn't listened.
Or maybe they hadn't allowed us to.

Now we were here.
At Michael Street.
Back in the fire.

And I couldn't help but wonder—how long before we turned to ash?

Chapter 19

When she didn't come home

Dread...

It was supposed to be a normal day. Just another Tuesday. Just another she walks home from Brownie's.

She wore her little uniform proudly, brown sash across her chest, patches not yet earned, her shoes double-knotted by our mother. She loved Brownies. It made her feel important, part of something. A sisterhood, they called it a sisterhood. But that night, sisterhood didn't save her.

She never made it home.

We didn't notice right away. Maybe because kids were always outside back then, riding bikes until dusk, running through yards, walking home from school without fear. But as the sun dropped, and the streetlights clicked on, we started looking. First with questions. Then with worry. Then, with full-blown panic.

Mom called out her name into the wind, over and over, like it would carry through the trees and lead her home. But there was no answer. Just silence. Just the sick feeling that something had gone terribly wrong.

Someone had taken her.

The man, as we would later learn, was much more than just a man. He was a predator. We can define a multiple murderer as someone who has committed multiple murders. A name familiar in courtrooms and on news broadcasts. A man with a history of hunting girls who looked just like her—innocent, trusting, full of light. He had already murdered other little girls by the time he found my sister. And now, she was in his hands.

We didn't know that yet, of course. All we knew was that our world had cracked in two.

When she finally came home—hours later, though it felt like years—she was alive. And that alone felt like a miracle. But something in her was gone. Stolen. Shattered. Her eyes, once wide and bright, now looked like they belonged to someone much older. Someone who had seen things no child should ever see.

Someone forced her to do unspeakable things. Things she didn't have words for.

Things that didn't belong in a child's life, or on a child's body.

And yet, she was still here. She had survived. And he had let her go.

Her selection was based on what criteria? Why not the others? Why had she come home when so many hadn't? We never got an answer. Maybe it was luck. Maybe it was divine mercy. Or maybe he just wanted to see if he could get away with letting one live.

But she was never the same.

None of us.

At first, people whispered. Not because they didn't care—but because they didn't know what to say. No one did. How do you speak to a seven-year-old kidnapped and returned with scars not on her skin, but on her soul? Type that is invisible. The kind you can't explain. The kind that doesn't bleed but never stops hurting.

She stopped talking for a while. Then when she did, she never said much. She used to giggle in the mornings. Dance while brushing her teeth. But after that night, she was quieter. More careful. She slept with the lights on. She didn't go near windows. And she never wanted to walk anywhere alone again.

And we—her siblings—watched it all unfold, helpless. Angry. Confused.

How could the world do that to someone so small? How could someone *choose* to hurt a child?

I was too young to understand the full picture, but old enough to feel it. Old enough to feel the air shift in our house. Old enough to know my sister wasn't safe, and neither was I, childhood didn't feel like a soft place anymore. It felt like a trapdoor.

They didn't let us talk about it. Not really. Not outside the house. Maybe people wanted to forget. Maybe it was too heavy. But silence became a second punishment. People expected my sister to carry this burden without faltering, and they expected us to ignore it.

But we saw it every day.
In her silence.
In her flinches.
In the way she folded into herself, even when sitting still.

My mother tried to be strong, but her hands shook more often. My father raged—not in protection, but in shame and fury, as if her being taken reflected on him. There was no therapy. No real healing. Just survive. Just a desperate attempt to move forward without falling apart.

They eventually caught the man who had taken her. His name made the news. There were mugshots, interviews, cold reports of his victims. They never publicly listed my sister's name. But we knew. We knew she had walked through the fire and somehow made it out the other side.

But survival comes at a price.

In the years that followed, she struggled. With confidence. Safely. With her own worth. And who could blame her? Someone dragged her out of childhood and threw her into darkness. And though she walked out, the dark followed.

She carried it in her bones.
In her addictions.
In her grief.
In the way she fought against a world that had once held her down and said, *you don't matter.*

She mattered.

She mattered to us. She was our sister to us. Our hero.
A survivor of something no child should have to

survive.
And she fought every day to keep going.

But the scars ran deep.

There are days I think about that uniform.
That sweet little Brownie sash.
And I wonder how different her life might have
been if the path home had stayed safe. If one man
hadn't reached into her life and torn it in half.

But I also remember this:

She came home.

Tattered. Hurt. Changed.
But she came home.

And though the world failed her, we never stopped
loving her.

Chapter 20

Hungry

Deprivation...

Hunger has a sound.

It starts as a quiet grumble in your belly, something you try to ignore. Then it grows louder, curling into your ribs, making your body feel heavy and hollow at the same time. But the worst part of hunger isn't in your stomach—it's in your heart. It's watching your brother stare at an empty cupboard. It's seeing your sister lick the last smear of peanut butter off a spoon and pretend she's full.

We were always hungry.

There were four of us. Kids trying to grow, trying to run and play like everyone else, while inside, we ached for something warm and filling. Our mom worked; She worked so hard. She worked wherever she could find it, waiting tables, cleaning, folding, and serving. To survive, she gave everything.

But it was never enough.

While she worked to support *us*, our father worked to support *himself*.

He earned money, but we didn't see it. It didn't go toward groceries or electricity or shoes with soles that held together. It went toward his cigarettes, his beer, his pride. He fed his appetite and left ours starving.

Most days, we didn't know where he was. He'd disappear for hours—sometimes days. When he came home, it was like a storm blowing through. Loud. Unpredictable. Angry that the house wasn't cleaner, the kids weren't quieter; the food wasn't hot—never mind that there *wasn't* food.

We stopped asking him for things.
We stopped trusting him to care.

So, we turned to each other.

We planned—quiet, desperate, and understood without speaking. If there were nothing in our kitchen, we'd knock on doors. One by one. Our neighbors weren't rich. They didn't live in fancy houses or drive new cars. But they had *something*. A loaf of bread. A slice of cheese. Cereal that came in a bag instead of a box. And most of them when they saw our faces—thin, dirty, hopeful— couldn't turn us away.

I remember standing on porches barefoot, twisting my fingers behind my back. My brother would do the talking. He had the bravest voice.

"Do you have anything to eat?"
"Just a sandwich?"
"Anything."

Sometimes it was a kind smile and a quick plate. Other times it was a sigh and a bag of old rolls. Once, a woman gave us leftover meatloaf wrapped in foil and said, "Don't tell your daddy I helped you." I didn't understand then why she whispered—but now I do.

There were also doors that didn't open. People who peeked through curtains and turned away. We didn't blame them. We just moved on.

We shared whatever we got. Even if it was one slice of bread, we tore it into four pieces. That was the rule. Nobody got more than anyone else. We were in this together. Every time.

My older sister used to make up games to distract us from the ache. She'd pretend we were in a contest—who could chew slower, who could make one cracker last the longest. My younger sister hummed when she was hungry. Soft, like a lullaby she made up to comfort herself.

We learned not to complain. Complaining didn't bring food. Complaining made things worse.

And we never told Mom. We couldn't. She was already drowning in guilt, in exhaustion, in shame she never deserved. We knew she was doing everything she could. She skipped meals for us. She worked double shifts, came home with cracked hands and blistered feet, and still kissed us goodnight.

She would've moved mountains for us. But she was stuck under one built by the man she married.

Dad would sometimes stroll in with fast food—just one bag. One burger. One soda. And he'd eat it in front of us. Smirking. Watching. Sometimes offering a single fry like it was a prize. We stopped looking at his food. We trained our eyes elsewhere. Because looking only made the ache worse.

I don't think he hated us. But he didn't *see* us.

He overlooked our protruding ribs and the way we gazed at empty plates. My brother's nightly tears, unseen by him, were unheard by all but me. He didn't see us at all—unless he needed someone to blame.

We learned to survive with little. A packet of saltine crackers and ketchup can create a meal. To savor powdered milk. To dream about peanut butter. Somehow, we found joy. We played a game. In the yard, we danced. We pretended the dry cereal was popcorn and watched the clouds as if they were cartoons.

But the hunger always came back.

It never really left.

Sometimes I still feel it, even now. Not just in my stomach—but in my soul. Panic sets in. That emptiness. That fear of needing and being too ashamed to ask. It lingers. Because when you grow up hungry, food is never just food. It's proof that you matter. That someone cares enough to keep you alive.

We kept each other alive.

Four little kids, knocking on doors, not because we were brave—but because we were starving. And because waiting for our father to come home with something real was like waiting for the moon to feed us.

It never happened.

Chapter 21

The House on Michael Street

Containment...

Michael Street.

Just a name to most people—but for us, it was a living thing. It let out a breath. A groan escaped. It watched. And sometimes, it felt like it was waiting. Waiting to see what would break next. Waiting to see which one of us would shatter first.

The house itself was small. Just two bedrooms— barely enough space for one family, let alone one with four kids and the weight of everything we carried. It had a small carport on the side, the kind you couldn't really park in without bumping the edge of the house. Cracks marred the concrete, and the posts leaned slightly, as if weary from years of excessive strain.

The yard was patchy. Dirt in places where grass had given up trying to grow. A chain-link fence surrounded it, but it never felt like it kept anything out—more like it kept us *in*.

When you walked through the front door, the air changed. Not because of the temperature, but because of the tension. It sat heavy in the air, like humidity you couldn't see but always felt. You learned to hold your breath a little, to listen for footsteps, to check expressions before speaking.

The living room was tight, with furniture that had seen better decades. A worn couch with broken springs. A recliner that leaned to one side. The carpet was dull, stained brown. The kind that never looked clean no matter how hard you scrubbed.

Down the narrow hallway, two bedrooms split off from each other. One for my parents. One for the rest of us. Four kids packed into a single room—sometimes two to a bed, sometimes one on the floor. We made nests out of blankets and pillows and called them forts. Not because it was fun, but because pretending helped. Pretending turned "no space" into "adventure."

There was one tiny bathroom. The kind where you had to move the shower curtain exactly right or water would spill everywhere. The faucet dripped no matter how tightly you turned the handle. Sometimes we fought over who got to go first in the morning, but most of the time, we didn't care. We just wanted hot water and a towel that didn't smell like mildew.

Tucked in the back like an afterthought, the kitchen was small. Cracks and curls marred the linoleum floor in places. Chips marred the cabinets. The fridge hummed too loudly. Sometimes it was full. Most times it wasn't. And when it was, it was because my mother had sacrificed something—usually herself by working her fingers to the bones.

That house heard everything.

It heard the yelling. The footsteps pounded down the hall. The cabinet doors slammed when anger had no place else to go. It heard the crying late at night, muffled into pillows. It heard the silence that came after—the kind that wasn't peaceful but full of things no one dared say out loud.

My father filled that house with fear.

He didn't have to raise his fist. His voice was enough. His presence. The way he'd throw open a door like a warning. The way his mood could sour a room before he even entered it. He controlled the temperature of that house—whether it burned with rage or froze with cold shoulders.

My mother filled it with quiet strength.

On most days, like a ghost, she moved through it silently, carefully avoiding trouble. When she could, she always did cleaning and cooking. She tucked us in. But you could see the weariness in her eyes. You could feel the sigh in her bones. She carried that house on her back, and it still wasn't enough to keep the walls from crumbling.

We tried to make it ours.

We put up drawings. During the Christmas season, we created paper chains. We blew out candles on birthday cakes made from a boxed mix. We laughed sometimes—quietly, nervously—like joy was a thing we had to steal when no one was looking.

But the house always knew.

It wasn't a home.
Not really.
It was a holding place. A cage with curtains. A stop on the road to survival.

The carport became our escape hatch. We'd sit out there on summer nights, hoping the breeze would bring peace. Sometimes we'd chalk the driveway. Other times, we'd just lie on our backs and stare at the stars, trying to imagine a world that felt bigger than this house.

We dreamed out there.
About different houses.

Bigger rooms.
Peaceful dinners.
Locks on the doors meant safety, not secrets.

Neighbors would pass by and nod. Some knew.
Some didn't. The ones who warned us not to move
in never said, "I told you so." They didn't have to.
We were living it.

Every corner of that house holds a memory.
Some good. Most not.

The hallway where we lined up for haircuts.
The wall we measured our heights against—
quietly, secretly.
The closet we hid in when the yelling got too loud.

Michael Street is just a street on a map. But for us,
it was a chapter. One filled with too much pain for
children to carry. And yet, we carried it. Together.
Barefoot, hungry, tired—but still standing.

We learned to live inside those walls.
And one day, we learned to walk away from them.

Chapter 22

Should We Go or Should We Stay

Crossroads...

My dad still lived with us

That question—*should we stay, or should we go?*—was never about geography. It wasn't about the street we lived on, or the number nailed to the mailbox. It was about survival. About safety. About peace. And no matter how many times we asked it, we never seemed to land on the answer we needed.

The truth is, we went.

We packed up the house on Michael Street, the same one where the walls held our screams and silence in equal measure, and we moved just two streets over to Jasper Street. Two streets. As if pain had boundaries. As if trauma had a zip code. As if changing addresses would change him.

It didn't.

He unpacked his same old rage in our new kitchen. Hung his anger in the hallway like a coat he never took off. The door slammed the same. The threats whispered through the walls the same. We weren't free. We had just moved the prison.

Jasper Street was supposed to be a fresh start. That's how my mom tried to paint it. "This house will be better," she said. "Smaller, quieter, simpler." But houses don't hold the magic to fix what's broken inside the people who live in them.

At first, we tried to believe it anyway. We rearranged furniture like it could rearrange our lives. My sisters and I picked our room and tried to make it our own. My brother stayed quiet, like he always did, but I caught him smiling once, like maybe this could be different.

But it wasn't.

It didn't take long. Maybe a few days. Maybe just a few hours.

He was still *him*.

The man who could suck the air out of a room with a look. The man who played the part of father when eyes were watching, and tyrant when they weren't. The man who knew how to keep us all tethered—by guilt, by fear, by false hope.

We'd wanted to believe in change. We clung to the idea that maybe *this* time he meant it. That maybe the fresh start would extend to his temper, his choices, his soul.

But abusers don't change because you change your curtains.

So, the question came back, louder this time: *Should we stay or should we go?*

We had gone—but not far enough.

Now we were trapped in a house we didn't yet hate, with a man we already did. We whispered more than we spoke. We walked lighter than before. Somehow, we became even quieter on Jasper Street than we had been on Michael. Because this time, we didn't have the excuse of "just waiting to leave." We *had* left—and it hadn't saved us.

The shame of that was its own weight.

I remember one night, my mom sat at the kitchen table long after we'd all gone to bed. I crept down the hall and peeked. She was holding a cup of coffee she wasn't drinking, staring through the window like the answers were written in the dark. I wondered if she was asking herself the same question. *Should I stay? Or go?* But she wasn't moving. None of us were.

We were paralyzed by the very man who should've protected us.

The thing is, leaving *with* him wasn't really leaving at all. It was just dressing the wound differently. And by moving to Jasper Street, we gave him more time. More room to plant roots in a place we hoped would heal us.

He made sure we remembered who was in charge.

He made sure we knew that this was *his* house now too.

He walked around like he owned it. His words punched harder in that cramped space. His anger bounced off the walls and wrapped around us like smoke—choking but invisible to anyone who didn't live inside it.

Still, we tried.

We tried to be normal. We invited friends over—carefully, only when he was away or calm. We cooked meals together. We laughed sometimes. We sat on the floor and played card games. But it always felt borrowed. Like any happiness we had was rented, and he'd come to collect.

And yet... something in us was shifting.

We had made *some* kind of move. Not far. Not free. But *different.*

That difference mattered.

It gave us a glimpse of what life *could* be, if only he wasn't in it. It gave us a taste of space. A sliver of courage.

Jasper Street wasn't our rescue—but it was our reckoning.

We began to see him more clearly. The charm he used to throw over us like a blanket started to wear thin. We could hear the lies as they fell from his mouth. We could see the patterns. The way he'd break us down, only to hold us hostage with guilt.

We were still afraid.

But now we were also *aware.*

And awareness, once it takes root, grows in all kinds of quiet ways. It grows in late-night talks between siblings. In locked doors. In the secret savings of babysitting money. In the refusal to flinch when his voice rose.

It grows in resolve.

We didn't leave right away. We didn't pack our bags and vanish. Life doesn't always work like that. Especially not when your father is the storm and the roof over your head at the same time.

But we were changing.

And eventually, *he* would be the one to go.

Not because he chose to. But because she finally did.

Chapter 23

The People we Could See

Corruption...

Across the street, there was another house.

What happened inside our home was only half the horror—because just beyond our walls, another kind of abuse was waiting, stalking children up and down our street in silence.

From the outside, it looked little different from ours. Modest. Worn. A sagging porch with uneven steps. Weeds grow up through the cracks in the sidewalk. A screen door that always seemed to slam.

We saw the girls out there sometimes—two of them, around our age. They played in the yard with stiff smiles and hollow laughter. Their movements always seemed careful, as if they were afraid of being watched, or worse, noticed.

And their father? He was always watching.

He sat on the porch in a rusted lawn chair. With smoke curling from his cigarette, a bottle tucked by his foot. He spoke to everyone. When he did, it was short, gruff, almost like a warning. But his eyes said more than his mouth ever did. Cold. Empty. Calculating.

Even as kids, we knew something was wrong.

It's strange how children can feel danger long before they understand it. It lives in the way someone moves. The tone of a voice. The silence between footsteps. We felt it in that house. We felt it when the screen door creaked open and those girls stepped outside, eyes on the ground, arms folded tightly across their chests.

They never talked much. Not to us. Not to anyone.

Sometimes we'd wave from the yard. One of them would wave back—timid, hesitant—before being called inside again. And every time that door closed behind them, it felt like a trapdoor shutting.

We didn't know the full truth then. But we knew enough.

Whispers floated around the neighborhood. First, in hushed tones. Then louder. Then, in the silence that confirms everything. People suspected. Some even said it out loud: *"He's messing with those girls."* But no one did anything. It was the 70s, so. Because no one wanted to get involved. Because

when you're poor and quiet and already broken,
the world doesn't care much about your pain.

And those girls? They didn't cry out for help.
Because who would've listened?

In houses like ours and theirs, one quickly learns
that some things are best left unsaid. The truth can
make things worse. That the people who are
supposed to protect you sometimes *are* the danger.
And that when your world is already on fire,
screaming only draws more heat.

Their father was their Goliath.
And no one was coming to save them.

We watched from our side of the street, hurting in
their own ways. Hungry. Afraid. Controlled. We
knew what it felt like to live in a house that didn't
feel like home. To walk on eggshells. To pretend
things were fine when they weren't. But what they
were living through… it was another kind of
prison.

We didn't talk about it. Not then.
But it haunted us.
Still does.

I remember one night seeing the older girl sitting
on the porch steps long after dark. She had her
arms wrapped around her knees and was rocking

slowly, staring at the gravel. She looked as if she were trying to disappear. Like if she rocked hard enough, she'd vanish into the night.

I wanted to go over. I wanted to ask if she was okay. But I was just a kid, too. And in that moment, I didn't have the words—or the courage.

We heard much later that the truth eventually came out. Not because someone stood up for them—but because the damage was already done. Years of it. Buried deep. One girl spoke up finally. And by then, it wasn't just about what had happened—but about what hadn't. What cannot they stop? What cannot they prevent?

By then, they were teenagers.
Changed.
Heavy with secrets they never should've carried.

Authorities arrested him, but not for long. The system didn't always know what to do with men like him. Men who hid their monsters behind locked doors and quiet daughters. Men who said things like, *"She made it up,"* or *"She's just acting out."*

And the neighborhood? It went quiet again. Just like before. Even with the truth revealed, people still struggle to respond.

We do.

We remember.

Across the street, in that tired house with peeling paint, girls were being hurt. And no one saved them. And sometimes, even now, I wonder how many other porches held the same secrets. How many other screen doors shut on cries that never made it past the hallway?

It changes how you look at people.
How you trust.
How you raise your own voice.

It teaches you that evil doesn't always roar. Occasionally, he smokes a cigarette. Sometimes, it fixes your bike. Sometimes, it calls itself *Daddy*.

And across the street from us, evil lived right out in the open.
And the world just kept turning.

Chapter 24

The neighborhood

Chaos...

People like to say, *"At least you had a roof over your head."*
But they never ask what kind of roof.
Or what you had to live through underneath it.

The neighborhood we grew up in was poor and occasionally not safe.
Not just because of what happened inside our own house—but because of what happened all around us. On the streets. Behind thin walls. Through open windows and broken fences. Fear didn't live in just one house. It lived in *every* direction.

Sirens were part of the soundtrack of our childhood.
Police lights flashed through our bedroom windows like strobe lights.
Shouting matches in the streets.
Dogs barking at things we didn't want to see.

It wasn't strange to see someone thrown against a car hood. It wasn't rare to see a child barefoot in the winter or a baby crying from a porch while adults fought inside. The brokenness was visible; It defined the landscape. And when you live in it long enough, you forget it's not normal.

Until something happens that reminds you how close you are to the edge.

I remember one afternoon—we were just inside, doing nothing. Maybe playing with old toys or fighting over a crust of bread. It was a normal day. And then suddenly everything changed.

The back door slammed open.

We all froze.

A woman burst through—sobbing, barefoot, wild-eyed. Her breath came in sharp gasps, and she didn't say a word. She didn't have to. The terror on her face said it all. She ran through the kitchen, past our mother, past us, and out the front door as fast as she'd come in.

And right behind her—her husband.

A man with murder in his eyes and a gun in his hand.

It happened so fast; It didn't feel real. One minute, we were kids trying to stretch out a bag of crackers, and the next, we were standing in the middle of someone else's war. My mother screamed at him to get out. We ducked behind furniture. My heart was beating so loud I thought it might explode.

He didn't stop. He kept going. Out the front door. After her.

We never heard a gunshot. Not that time. But the sound of that back door slamming open— of terror crashing into our already fragile peace— stayed with me forever.

That's what our neighborhood was like. You never knew when danger would come crashing through.

You couldn't ride your bike too far without someone shouting something nasty. You couldn't leave your toys outside—they'd be gone by morning. Sometimes you'd hear glass breaking two doors down. Sometimes people screamed all night. Once, I saw a man drag his wife by the hair down the front steps of their house like it was nothing.

And still—we stayed.

Because where do you go when you have nowhere else?

Where do you run when the entire world feels like one long hallway with no exit?

Cracks marred the streets. The paint peeled off houses like sunburned skin. Most of the curtains stayed drawn all day long, and you learned not to ask why. The corner store had bars on the windows. The streetlights flickered as if they were too tired to stay on.

And the people? They were tired too.

You could see it on their faces. Everyone was just trying to make it. Trying to keep the lights on. Trying to raise kids in places that stole their innocence like loose change. No one had time to look out for anyone else. Everyone was busy surviving.

Even the kids changed.

They stopped being kids too soon.
We all did.

You learn to watch everything. Who's walking by? What car hasn't moved in three days? Which houses to avoid. Learning: You learn to freeze at the sound of yelling. You learn how to disappear when things get too loud. You learn how to blend in with the pain, so you don't stick out and get swallowed by it.

But that moment—the woman with the gun behind her—ripped through even our toughest armor.

Because if someone could run *through* our house like that, what else could come in? We already didn't feel safe inside our own walls—but that day, it felt like there were no walls at all.

We asked our mom what had happened.
She didn't have answers.

She just locked the door behind them and sat down hard at the kitchen table, her hands trembling. That silence afterward—the kind that hums through your bones—was worse than any shouting.
Because in that silence, we knew it could happen again.

Anytime.

Anywhere.

And it wasn't just the neighbors.
It was a neighborhood.
It was the system.
It was a trap of poverty, violence, silence, and shame.

We didn't choose it.
We were born into it.

And for too long, we thought that was all there was.

But it wasn't.

Later—years later—I'd live in a place where doors didn't slam with fear behind them. Where police sirens didn't make my heart race. Where people smiled because they meant it, not because they were hiding something behind their teeth. And it would hit me all over again:

That neighborhood wasn't normal.
That fear wasn't supposed to be constant.
That we were never safe there—not really.

But somehow, we survived it.
One slammed door at a time.
One broken night after another.

And I've never forgotten what it felt like the day danger didn't just knock—
It ran straight through.

Chapter 25

Locked Doors

Fear...

Some people lock doors out of habit.
I lock mine out of *survival*.

It's the first thing I do when I walk into a room.
Slide the bolt. Turn the key. Check the knob twice,
sometimes three times, just to make sure. At night,
before I sleep, I do a round—front door, back door,
windows, even closet doors. I don't rest until I've
secured everything.

Safe.

But here's the truth: I never really feel safe. I just
feel *less exposed*.

That started young. I first grasped back then that
the world hadn't protected kids like me. Back
when I understood, long before I had the words for
it, that danger wasn't some faraway thing—it was
just on the other side of a door.

At Michael Street and the houses after, danger
didn't always knock. Sometimes it just walked

right in. Sometimes it *was* already inside. And when it wasn't, it came from outside—from the street, the neighbors, the yelling, the chaos that crept in like smoke no matter how tightly we shut the windows.

I remember the day the woman ran through our house.
Back door to front door.
Sobbing.
Barefoot.
Her husband was chasing her with a gun.

We didn't know her name. But in that moment, she used our house like a tunnel—an escape route through someone else's nightmare. And for those few terrifying seconds, we were in it too. Watching violence pass through our living room like wind.

Afterward, my mother locked the door.
But it was too late.
The damage was done.

From that day on, I learned that a locked door could mean the difference between witnessing terror—and being swallowed by it.

And yet, in our house, doors didn't always mean safety.

My father had keys. And when he didn't use them, he used his voice. His footsteps. His fists were against the wall. Even when the door closed, we knew he could walk in whenever he wanted.

There were no boundaries he respected. No privacy. No pause. He made his presence known in every room, even when he wasn't physically in it. We tiptoed around the house as if we were trespassers in our own lives. Holding our breath. Listening for cues. Waiting for the mood to shift.

I started sleeping with the blanket pulled to my chin, like fabric could save me. I'd listen to every creak of the floor, every whisper through the wall. And when I got old enough to understand what locks were for—I used them every chance I got.

But they didn't always allow that.

He hated locked doors. Said it meant we were hiding something. He'd shout, bang, threaten to take them off the hinges. Because control can't tolerate boundaries. And in his mind, we weren't people. We were property.

Still, I locked them when I could. Even if it meant getting yelled at. Even if it meant waiting until I heard him leave the house. It was the only thing I could do to feel like I had *some* power.

145

A locked door became my line in the sand.

Years passed. We left that neighborhood. Left that street. Left him.

But the fear didn't stay behind.

Even now, long after I've grown, long after I've built a life of my own, I still check the locks. Even during the day, I still bolt the door. I keep my bedroom closed tight. I still jump when someone knocks unexpectedly. And when I hear footsteps outside or see a strange car parked too long near my home, my heart races like I'm right back on that porch, watching that woman flee for her life.

People laugh sometimes.
"You're so paranoid," they say.
"Relax. Nothing's going to happen."

But how do you explain to someone who never lived it?

How do you tell them that safety isn't a given—
it's something you *fight* for?
That peace of mind isn't peace at all—its vigilance wrapped in calm?
That for kids who grew up in chaos, safety isn't a state—it's a performance?

Your eyes scan the room. Always keep your back against the wall for protection. You memorize exits. You plan what you'd do if someone broke in, if someone raised their voice, if someone started reaching for something that looked like a weapon.

All from the outside, it looks like hypervigilance. From the inside, it feels like staying alive.

Locked doors are my armor now.

They remind me that I have a choice. That I get to decide who comes in. That I am no longer that child waiting for the storm. That I can create spaces where chaos isn't welcome.

It's not about paranoia.
It's about boundaries.
It's about reclaiming something I could never have as a child—*control*.

There are still nights I can't sleep until I've checked everything twice. Still, there are days when a loud knock sends my body into a spiral of old memories. A cracked door still makes me nervous.

But I remind myself:
I'm not there anymore.

I'm not powerless.
I survived it.

And now?
Now, I lock the door *because I can*.

Chapter 26

Four Doors Down

Realization…

Moving again wasn't unusual. By the time I was old enough to know what "home" should feel like, the word had already lost its meaning. But this move was different—not across town, not out of state, not even to a new school zone. This time, it was just four houses down.

It should have felt simple, like a change in furniture. The street was identical. Same cracked sidewalk. Same neighbors pretending not to notice the chaos spilling from our front porch. But even four houses down, everything changed. This one my parents owned

The new house was older, quieter. It had a strange smell—damp wood and something that reminded me of dust-covered memories. The floorboards creaked with secrets. The wallpaper peeled at the corners as if it wanted to whisper. But it was the silence that pressed hardest. There were no arguments from the other side of the wall. No TV hummed through the thin sheetrock. Just an eerie calm.

And then we found the space.

It wasn't a room; Instead, it was something else. It wasn't even on the blueprint the landlord gave us. A built-in cabinet in the bathroom hid it. An oddly narrow piece of furniture that didn't quite fit the aesthetic of the rest of the house. One day, while exploring, my brother yanked the bottom drawer out completely and noticed something unusual there.

He stuck his fingers into the gap and pulled. With effort, the back panel came loose, revealing a crawl-sized hole, no higher than our waists. Behind it: darkness. But the kind that doesn't just fill a space—it watches.

We didn't tell our parents. The last thing we needed was Dad turning the space into one of his twisted punishments or locking us in for "time-outs" that could last until he remembered we existed. So instead, we kept it between us—our secret.

Inside the hidden space, the walls were unfinished. Dust covered the exposed beams. There was old newspaper clippings pinned to the studs, yellowed and curled at the edges. Names we didn't recognize. Headlines like *"Local Girl Still Missing"* and *"Family of Four Vanishes—No Suspects."* We also found old alcohol bottles that still reeked of the smell that originally occupied the space. My sister said it was just storage. My brother said it was a hiding place. I thought it felt like a memory of someone trying to bury alive.

We started hearing things at night.

No footsteps, not a creak. Those were normal in an old house. These were different. They were... patterns. Rhythmic taps on the floor. A knock, pause, knock-knock. A shuffle like someone dragging something heavy, followed by complete silence. It's always between two and three in the morning. The hour when nightmares take their first breath.

I made the mistake of mentioning it to my mom once. She brushed it off with, "Old houses settle weird." But her eyes darted toward the bathroom cabinet as she said it. And that's when I knew— she heard it too.

One night, the tapping didn't stop. It went on for nearly twenty minutes, followed by what sounded like whispering through the vent. No words. Not at first. Just... breathy syllables. My brother pressed his ear to the wall and said he could hear someone saying, "Still here."

We blocked the crawlspace entrance with books and boxes, but they'd fall over by morning. No one touched them. No one admitted to hearing more.

Then came the dreams.

My sister woke up screaming one night, said she saw a man standing at the end of our hallway, just outside the crawlspace. Dad wasn't awake; He had passed out on the couch. This man was tall, motionless. He tilted his head as if listening. She said she couldn't move. Said his eyes were open too wide, too still. When she blinked, he was gone.

We chalked it up to stress. God knows we had plenty. But the dreams kept coming.

For me, it was always the same: I'd crawl into the hidden space, except it kept going. Longer and longer, until I couldn't turn around. Then I'd hear my name. But not from one voice—from all of them. Every missing person on those yellowed clippings whispered, "Come closer."

Why we stayed in that house? Because we always stayed. Abuse was normal. Fear was on a Tuesday. And hidden spaces were safer than the open ones.

At least in there, the ghosts didn't slap you across the mouth or throw chairs through windows.

Still, the house took its toll.

We knew we had to leave. We just didn't know how.

Every time we mentioned moving, Dad shut it down. Said it was the "only house that didn't betray him." That made little sense—until we realized what he meant.

He wasn't afraid of the house. He was part of it.

He was aware of the cabinet space. He always knew. And maybe... just maybe, whatever lived in that crawlspace wasn't just haunting us. Maybe it was haunting him too.

And so, this is where the rest of the story takes place—not in a house, but in a space just out of sight. A place where fear fermented. A place that listened to every word spoken as it waited in silence.

Four doors down.

And deep, deep within.

Chapter 27

The Floor Moved

Shock...

It was somewhere between midnight and madness when I woke up.

The night where time folds in on itself—no ticking clock, no sound but breath. I lay there, frozen, the stale air thick with that mildew-and-metal smell that only this house could create. The air felt wrong. It always did when *it* was near.

At first, I thought it was a dream. My eyes fluttered open, the dark pressing down around me like a wet blanket. But the feeling in my chest told me it was real—too real. Something wasn't right.

The floor moved.

It was a subtle rustle at first. Soft scratching like tiny claws against the wood. Then came the clicking—quick, scattered. I lifted my head, heart pounding. And that's when I saw them.

Dozens of them.

Rats.

They weren't running in a frenzy like you'd expect. They marched, organized, from one corner of the room to the other. Their beady eyes glowed faintly in the moonlight that sliced through the window. Their long pink tails dragged behind them like threads unraveling from a cursed blanket.

I wanted to scream, but no sound came out. I blinked hard—once, twice—but they didn't disappear. One rat stopped near the bunk bed and turned its head toward me, like it knew I was watching. Its nose twitched. It stood still for a second, then crawled beneath the lower bunk, disappearing into the shadows.

I squeezed my eyes shut. "This isn't real," I whispered.

But when I opened them again, something far worse greeted me.

Snakes.

Not on the floor. On the *walls*.

They slithered around the edges of the door frame, their long bodies gliding in slow, deliberate arcs. One wrapped around the light switch, tongue flicking toward me. Another snake coiled above the door, its skin a sickly green with patches of red, as if dipped in blood.

The sight paralyzed me.

This wasn't just a nightmare—it was a message.

Something evil had taken root in this house. I'd felt it in the crawlspace. Heard it in the tapping on the walls. But now... now it was making itself known in the open. It wanted me to see. To fear. To break.

I pulled my blanket up to my chin and tried not to move. The mattress creaked beneath me as if it might give me away. From the top bunk, I heard my sister stirring. "Did you hear that?" I whispered.

She didn't answer. I stared at the snakes circling the doorframe as if guarding it. Or trapping us in.

A rat darted out from beneath the bed, pausing just long enough for me to see something glinting between its teeth. It was holding a piece of broken glass. My breath hitched. I didn't know what that meant, but it felt like a symbol—something meant to hurt. Something meant to warn.

My brother's voice came from the far side of the room. "I don't see anything?"

I nodded even though he couldn't see me. There was a smell sharp and bitter—like burnt rubber and rot. It curled through the air like a gas leak from hell. I buried my face in my pillow, trying not to gag.

We didn't speak again. It wasn't necessary. We were all awake. All watching but they didn't see what I saw.

And whatever was in the house was watching me back.

The snakes didn't strike. They didn't hiss. They didn't move any faster than a slow glide. But there was intelligence in their eyes. I swear it. I don't care what anyone says about dreams or trauma. These things had a *purpose*.

One snake tilted its head toward the bunk bed. My fists clenched under the blanket. I remembered every story I'd been told growing up about evil spirits and demons. About how they sometimes appear as animals. About how they come in shadows, in silence.

That night, both filled the room.

I wanted to cry, but I couldn't risk making a sound. The rats had circled again. Their claws tapped in a rhythmic loop that didn't match any natural movement. It was… ritualistic. Almost like a chant made of motion.

And then it stopped.

All at once.

The rats froze. The snakes turned toward the window. And in the blink of an eye—gone.

Nothing moved.

The air was still. The house returned to its silence, as if it had inhaled and held its breath. My heart kept hammering in my chest, unsure if the worst was over or just beginning.

My brother slipped out of bed and crawled over beside me. "What did you see?" he whispered.

I shook my head. I didn't know.

But I knew this: the house had changed.

That night, the evil in the walls had shown us a piece of itself. Just a glimpse. A warning. And it was enough.

I never mentioned the rats or the snakes again. Not aloud.

But every night after that, I double-checked the corners. I stared at the doorway before I let myself sleep. And when the moonlight hit exactly right, I could still see the shadows where they once slithered.

Something in the house had awakened.

And now I feared it was inside us too.

Chapter 28

The Boy in the Window

Watcher...

I don't remember what woke me that night. Maybe it was the creak in the old wood beneath the house. Maybe the wind whispered secrets through the cracked frame is what I heard. Alternatively, it may have been an underlying intuition—an unspoken awareness that an event was imminent.

The room was chilly. Not the cold you can fix with a blanket, but the kind that seeps into your bones and makes you feel smaller than you already are. I sat up in bed and looked across the room. My siblings were still sleeping—curled into themselves like they were trying to disappear.

I didn't blame them. Some nights, vanishing seemed peaceful.

That's when I saw him.

A flicker in the dark, just beyond the window. A boy. At first, I thought I was dreaming—or maybe still asleep. He stood outside, just beyond the reach of the porch light, where shadows danced on the edge of real and pretend.

He looked young, maybe my age. Same height. Same messy hair. He wasn't moving, just standing there… watching.

My heart skipped. Every story I'd ever heard about prowlers and strangers came rushing back. But something about him felt different. Not dangerous. Not quite.

He wore clothes that looked out of place—like something out of a storybook. A loose shirt that flared at the sleeves and pants that were a little too short, like he'd grown up too fast but hadn't gotten new clothes. On his head sat the shadow of a cap, tilted to the side. He wore scuffed shoes. He stood with his feet pointed, poised to leap at any moment.

For a moment, I thought: *Peter Pan.*

It sounds silly now; I know. But when you're a child in a house filled with fear, you cling to anything that looks like freedom. Peter Pan was a boy who didn't grow up. Who flew away from pain? Who had friends and magic and stars?

And for one breathless second, he'd come for me.

I slipped off the bed, careful not to wake anyone, and crept to the window. My breath fogged the glass as I leaned in. He didn't move. Just looked at me with eyes that weren't wide with curiosity or wild with mischief.

They were… kind.

Soft.

Sad, maybe.

And in that look, I felt something shift in me.

I blinked. He was still there.

I opened the window just a crack to feel the night air kiss my skin. It wasn't as cold as before. It was warmer now. Safe.

"Are you real?" I whispered.

He didn't answer.

"Are you… him?"

I mean Peter Pan. I don't know why I said it. Maybe I hoped if I said the name aloud, he'd nod and say, *yes, and I'm taking you to Neverland.*

But he didn't nod. He didn't speak.

162

And still—I knew.

That wasn't Peter Pan.

That was something great.

Something sent.

Something divine.

It wasn't until I felt the warmth spread across my chest that I understood. The fear I carried like a backpack full of bricks slipped off me in that moment. The weight of every scream, every slammed door, every night I cried into a pillow—it felt it melt.

He wasn't there to take me away.

He was there to remind me I wasn't alone.

I don't know how long we stared at each other. Time didn't work right that night. But when I blinked again, he was gone.

No footsteps.

No goodbye.

Just… gone.

Gripping the windowsill, I stood and let the quiet fill the space he'd left. I wasn't unhappy. No sense of abandonment washed over me. I felt... protected. Watched over. Like someone had been keeping score of every moment I thought no one saw.

The next morning, I didn't tell anyone. How do you explain something like that? You don't.

But I knew what I saw.

I thought it was my secret to keep. Later, my brother mentioned he had seen me talking out the window and heard me say *Peter Pan*.

As the days wore on, whenever things got hard— when the yelling started, or the walls seemed too close, or the dark wrapped too tightly around us— I'd look out that window.

I never saw him again.

But I felt him.

Every time I needed to be brave, every time I shielded my siblings, or took the blame so we could sleep a little longer in peace or stood between pain and someone smaller—I felt that warmth return.

Maybe he *was* Peter Pan. Maybe he was something else. An angel. A guardian. A piece of me that still believed in good things.

Whoever he was, he changed me.

And in a house full of nightmares, he became my light.

Chapter 29

Biscuits and Gravy

Escape...

Time does not paint every memory in shadows.

Sometimes, when I close my eyes and let my mind drift past the chaos and fear, I land softly on a warm kitchen floor. A place where the world slowed down, and for a little while, everything felt okay. That place was just across the street.

Her name was Ruby. A good friend in those days. Her house was old, like ours, but it felt different inside. Lighter. Happier. The air always smelled like comfort—fresh biscuits, sizzling sausage, a pot of gravy bubbling on the stove, and a little sweetness from jelly jars lined up like trophies.

Ruby's grandma was the one who made it all. She was stout, with soft cheeks and a voice that hummed instead of speaking. She wore aprons that had stories stitched into them, and she moved like she knew what every day needed. Her kitchen was always warm, not just from the oven, but from the way she treated us—like we mattered.

We'd tiptoe in, hair wild and eyes barely open, still in our sleep shirts. She'd hand us tiny glass cups of orange juice like we were royalty and say, "Morning, sweet babies," as if we were her own. We'd giggle and sit at the table, legs swinging, waiting for those plates.

Biscuits and gravy.

If heaven has a scent, I'm convinced it smells just like that kitchen.

We ate slowly, not because we had to but because we wanted to make it last. Ruby and I would whisper about our plans for the day while steam curled from our plates. It was never anything grand—just dolls and songs and dreams of pop stars who didn't know we existed but who, in our world, were already our husbands.

Ruby was married to Donny Osmond. I was married to Tony DeFranco. Sometimes we'd switch just for drama, like the time we both fought over Leif Garrett and refused to speak for an hour. Eventually, her grandma told us, "Girls, you best not waste your whole life waiting on boys who don't know how to cook breakfast," and we laughed so hard we forgot we were mad.

We'd spend hours on her porch with Barbies scattered everywhere, making up wild adventures.

167

Our dolls lived in castles made from shoeboxes, and their weddings had guest lists of rock stars and movie idols. We wore our mama's old slips as gowns, tucked flowers behind our ears, and sang wedding songs with all the emotion our little hearts could carry.

Sometimes her grandma would come out with a pitcher of Kool-Aid and a plate of peanut butter crackers and say, "You two sure got good imaginations." We did. Because we had to.

Inside my home, things weren't always soft. But across the street, I had a place for pretending, where fear didn't echo in the laughter, and where we celebrated a little girl's dreams.

When Ruby and I tired of dolls, we'd play hopscotch on the sidewalk or climb into the tree out front with a bag of candy we bought from the corner store. We'd sit in the branches and talk about what life would be like when we were famous. I was going to be a singer. She was going to be a dancer on *The Lawrence Welk Show*. We believed it with all our hearts.

Sometimes her grandma would call us in just to brush our hair. She had this old pink brush with a missing bristle, and she'd sit us down one at a time on a kitchen chair and run it through our tangles.

"A girl's got to feel cared for," she'd say. And we did.

I didn't realize until years later how rare that was—how important. That a grandmother, not even mine, took the time to make two little girls feel seen, fed, and safe.

One morning stands out above all the others. It was cold, and the windows were foggy on the inside. At the kitchen table, Ruby and I huddled in blankets while her grandma stirred gravy. She looked out the window and said, "Y'all keep each other close, all right? The world's hard sometimes. But you've got each other."

We nodded, not really understanding. But we remember.

That day, she gave us each of us advice. Nothing we thought we needed to know, but she told us we were lucky. Said if we ever felt lost, we should hold on to our hearts and remember the mornings that started with biscuits, dolls, and pop star husbands.

I kept those thoughts for years. Taped it inside a notebook full of doodles, lyrics, and daydreams. When things got dark, I'd open that notebook and feel the kitchen warmth all over again.

Sometimes, people think you must go far to find angels.

They live across the street.

In kitchens redolent with the aroma of biscuits and gravy. In women who call you "sweet baby" and brush your hair with a pink-handled brush. In little girls who share Kool-Aid, dream big, and never let go of each other, even if life pulls them in different directions.

That house is still there. The porch, the tree, the smell of breakfast—just a memory.

But when I think back to my childhood, it's not always the fear, the noise, or the hurt that surfaces first.

Sometimes, it's the laughter.

The sweetness.

The dolls are in wedding gowns.

And a grandma who gave me a place to just be a little girl.

Chapter 30

The Boy Next Door

Shadowed...

Every neighborhood has *that* kid—the one who rides his bike too fast, laughs too loud, climbs too high, and somehow always gets into just enough trouble to be entertaining, but not mean. For us, that kid was Scott. The boy next door.

Scott was my brother's best friend. They were inseparable, like peanut butter and jelly, or thunder and lightning—where you found one, the other wasn't far behind. Scraped knees, inside jokes, and whispered plans beneath summer stars stitched together their friendship.

Scott had a wild mop of brown hair and a grin that was pure mischief. You could see the next idea forming behind his eyes before he even opened his mouth. He always had something brewing—a shortcut through the woods, a plan to build a fort with cardboard and string, or a daring stunt involving a bike ramp and a cinder block.

My brother and Scott could turn anything into an adventure. A ditch became a battlefield. A pile of leaves was a hidden treasure. An old refrigerator box transformed into a spaceship. They were creators of worlds, supporters of make-believe, and fearless in their pursuits—even when those pursuits meant running from an angry neighbor after accidentally knocking over a flowerpot.

Scott wasn't a bad kid—simply curious. Bold. He wanted to feel the wind in his face and the thrill in his chest. He had no interest in being told *no,* and rules were more like soft suggestions to him. That caused frustration for some adults. But we loved him for it. He made life electric.

And even when he pushed the limits, he never left my brother behind. They were a team. If Scott got caught sneaking cookies, my brother would take the blame. If my brother scraped his arm climbing a tree, Scott would be the one who carried him home.

I remember one afternoon. They had discovered a nest of baby squirrels in a tree and spent the entire day watching over them like tiny woodland parents. Scott even tried to feed them crackers. He thought maybe, just maybe, they'd grow up and follow him around like pets. That was Scott's kind of thinking—optimistic, creative, a little outrageous, and full of heart.

But time doesn't pause for magic, even for boys like Scott.

It happened on a day that should've been ordinary. I can still hear the echo of that ladder tipping. The silence that followed was heavier than any scream.

My mom told us that a knock came at her door.

Scott had fallen—just trying to fix something, or maybe reach something, or maybe just being Scott, trying to climb higher than he should have. He was older then and it happened at work. All we knew was that our boy next door was gone.

He was too young. *Way* too young.

And the world suddenly felt quieter.

My brother didn't speak for days. He wouldn't eat much either. He just sat in their usual spots—by the tree where they watched squirrels, on the front step where they made plans, in the yard where they had raced each other a hundred times—and stared. He thought maybe Scott would come back. That was just one more trick. But tricks end. Some holes remain unfilled.

The thing about a kid like Scott is he leaves more than memories behind. He leaves *motion*. A spark. And when he's gone, you feel it—not just the absence of the person, but the quiet where all the laughter used to be.

At Scott's funeral, they played a song he used to hum all the time. One of those songs that gets stuck in your head even though you don't know the name. The pastor said he was a man "full of light and spirit." I thought that was perfect.
He *was* light. He flared. Too bright, maybe, for a world that didn't always know what to do with a man like that.

My brother carried a piece of Scott with him since his death. He still talks about him sometimes. In the way people do when a memory is both heavy and sweet. He'll laugh about the prank Scott pulled or the way he used to chew the ends of his pencils. But I can see it in his eyes—that ache. He left that space behind.

And I carry Scott with me, too. Every time I see a boy with scraped knees and dirt on his hands; I think of him. Every time I see kids racing down the street on bikes, hair wild and hearts unafraid, I smile. Because that was Scott.

The boy next door.

The boy who believed cardboard could be a
spaceship.

The boy who made us all feel braver just by being
in his orbit.

And even now, after all these years, I like to
believe he's still climbing up into the sky this time,
not to reach fruit or build something new, but just
to be closer to the stars. Where mischief is just
another word for wonder, and men who left too
soon get to keep flying.

Chapter 31

Birthday Switches

Humiliation...

Most children look forward to their birthdays with excitement—a cake with frosting, candles to blow out, a small, wrapped present or two, and the warm feeling of being celebrated just for existing. For us, birthdays didn't come with balloons or joy. They came with something far darker. Something that still lingers like a shadow over the idea of getting older.

In our house, a birthday wasn't a celebration. It was a punishment.

There was no party, no laughter, no special treat. Instead, it began with a simple command that filled us with dread: "Go outside and get a switch."

Instead, it's not just any branch. Not too thick. Not too thin. It had to be *exactly right*—long enough to sting, thin enough to whistle through the air. We learned to search the yard with numb hands and heavy hearts. The same tree that gave us shade in the summer, the one we played under with our bare feet in the dirt, was the place we harvested our own pain.

He made us pick our own switches.

There was something cruel in that ritual. A humiliation that seeped deep into our skin even before the first strike. Knowing what was coming, knowing we were about to be hurt—on the very day we were supposed to be cherished—was a weight too heavy for a child to carry.

We would line up, in the little room we all shared. He would sit in his chair, the switch in his hand, inspecting it like a judge before sentencing. His expression never changed—stern, cold, as if this was simply what had to be done.

Then the whipping would begin.

Instead, his actions lacked both speed and symbolism. It was harsh. It was full of rage. As if he resented us for being born. As if each birthday was a reminder of his obligations, his disappointments, his lost freedom. The switch cracked through the air and lashed across our legs, our arms, sometimes our backs. The tears came quickly, the cries even faster. But mercy never did.

He hit us as if we were mistakes.

As if we had no right to exist.

Like our very existence demanded punishment.

There was no safe word. No gentle voice to follow. No mother to shield us. She tried sometimes, but she had her own bruises, her own battles. And on our birthdays, even she seemed smaller, quieter, trying to keep the peace that never came.

I remember one birthday. Around six or seven, that's when it happened. I had woken up early, hoping—just *hoping*—maybe this year would be different. Maybe I'd get a hug. Maybe he'd smile. But by mid-morning, the command came.

"Get the switch."

That day, I took too long. I wandered around the yard trying to delay the inevitable. Looking up at the branches, wondering what I did wrong. Why was being born such an offense? Why I had to suffer just for existing.

When I finally brought one back, he was already angry.

"Trying to hide?" he snapped. "Trying to make it worse for yourself?"

And worse it became.

That switch broke before he was done, so he went outside to get another. He made me wait. Standing there. Tears hot on my face. Shame burned deeper than any wound.

Afterward, I curled up on the thin mattress in the room, trying to be small, trying not to breathe too loudly. My siblings were just as broken beside me. Silence hung between us. We didn't cry aloud anymore. We just lay there, soaking in the silence and the pain.

Happy birthday to us.

The irony is he never forgot a birthday. He remembered every single one. Not to buy a gift or make a cake, but to remind us—**you are mine to hurt.**

It wasn't until much later in life that I learned this wasn't normal. Other kids: Other children were not required to cut their own switches. They got presents and kisses and parties with friends. That they blew out candles on cakes, not bruises on skin.

The memories have stayed with me. And for a long time, I dreaded the day of my birth. I didn't tell people when it was. No celebration happened for me. I didn't want anyone to look at me, to acknowledge a day that was only ever marked by pain.

I carried the message he gave us in those beatings: **You should never have been born.**

But I *was* born.

And I survived.

And now I know better.

I know that love doesn't strike. Birthdays: Birthdays deserve to be treated as sacred. That children should feel adored, not afraid. That, in my story, though marked by cruelty, is mine to reclaim.

These days, when my birthday comes, I light a candle—not just for the year I've lived, but for every year I've endured. Every year I proved him wrong. Every year I stayed, grew, and loved anyway.

And I remember my siblings—those small warriors beside me in that little shared room. We survived those birthday switches. And we found ways, somehow, to grow into our own lives, our own stories, our own freedom.

We picked switches once.

Now, we pick healing.

Chapter 32

Who Ate the Cherry

Blame...

The worst dreams weren't the ones that came
while we slept.
They were the ones we woke up in.

Sometimes it started with the creak of a door, or
the sudden slam of a cabinet. Other times, it was
his voice—low and sharp, already angry. But most
often, it was the jolt of being pulled out of sleep
with the same sinking feeling in our
stomachs: *He's doing it again.*

We never knew what time it was when it
happened—only that the world outside was still
dark, the air in the house still thick, and our hearts
still pounding before our eyes were even fully
open. Someone woke us one by one and lined us
up like suspects in a crime we didn't commit.

Half-asleep, barefoot, and blinking in confusion,
we'd stand shoulder to shoulder in our pajamas in
the narrow hallway. A line of scared children, still
warm from bed, faced a man whose rage didn't
care what hour it was.

He would pace. Bark questions. Accuse. Throw open cabinets and point to items as though they held the evidence he needed to prove we were guilty of something.

"Where's the remote?!"
"Who moved my cigarettes?!"
"Who ate one of my cherries?!"

The cherries. That night still lives in my bones.

There was a bag in the fridge—bright red fresh and glowing like rubies. Off-limits. *His*. Just like the TV, the cigarettes, the air we breathed.

We knew better than to touch them. But someone had. Or maybe he just thought someone had. That was the thing about him: he didn't need proof. He needed only a suspicion. The idea of disobedience was enough to become truth in his eyes.

He had *counted* them. That's what he said, over and over. "I counted them, and one is gone." His voice was quiet, like the eye of a storm. That was always worse than shouting.

He pointed at each of us. "Who ate the cherry?"

No one spoke.

Not because we were guilty, but because we were *terrified*. Because the wrong word could set him off. Because the only answer he wanted was a confession, and none of us could give it.

So, I always did what I did when the silence became unbearable.

I lied.

"I did," I whispered.

His head snapped toward me. "You did?"

I nodded barely. My voice trembled. "Yes."

I didn't. But I knew what would happen if no one confessed. The night would go on. We would stand there until our legs ached. Someone would get slapped. Someone would get blamed anyway. The rage would look for a home, and it would find one. Better than me, I figured. Better I lie and end it.

He scowled. Told me how ungrateful I was. How worthless. How stupid. I stared at the floor, taking the words like punches. And then eventually, he turned and went back to his room, slamming the door.

He dismissed us. Not with comfort. Not with understanding. Just silence.

We went back to our little room—four of us crammed into one space—and tried to sleep again. But sleep didn't come easily. It never did after nights like that.

Because it wasn't just the cherries.
It was always something.

Sometimes it was a cigarette lighter he couldn't find. Sometimes the TV remote. Once, it was a single sock. And always, there was the same routine: the line, the accusations, the feeling that we were being punished simply for existing.

The line in the hallway became a symbol of our childhood.
We were never truly safe—not even in sleep.
Not even as children.
Not even in our own beds.

There was no logic in it. No fairness. No way to win. He had turned our home into a courtroom, and he was judge, jury, and executioner. And we were always on trial.

It made us grow up fast.

Hiding things, including both objects and emotions, was something we learned. We learned to expect his moods like weather reports. We learned the art of silence. The power of a lie told to protect a sibling. The heartbreak of seeing someone you love getting punished just for being in the wrong place at the wrong time.

And we learned how to survive.

But survival isn't living. It's treading water while pretending not to drown.

The cherries never left my mind. Not because of the cherry itself—but because of what it represented: the way he needed control over everything. Our food is also part of the price. Even our sleep. Even our thoughts.

He counted the cherries because he needed to count *us*.
To keep track of every move. Every breath. Every mistake.

Years later, I still flinch when someone turns on a light in the middle of the night. I still can't look at cherries without feeling that icy grip in my chest. And sometimes, I still wake in the dark, half expecting to hear my name barked from down the hallway.

But I don't live there anymore.

Now, I live in a house where midnight means rest. Instead, we don't wake anyone unless it's for a gentle hug or a bad dream. Where cherries are just cherries. Where children can consume them freely. Where the only things lined up at night are slippers by the bed.

He took so much from us.
But he didn't get everything.

He didn't get our kindness.
He didn't get our empathy.
He didn't get our ability to break the cycle.

We're still here.
We still stand in a line—shoulder to shoulder—but now it's at reunions. On holidays. In photos where we smile not because we must, but because we *mean it*.

And if someone asks who ate the last cherry now?

We laugh. Shrugging, we respond. Did we say, "Who cares? There's more in the Fridge."

And then we go on living.

Chapter 33

The Great Escape

Freedom...

Sometimes survival isn't just about staying. It's about *leaving*.

My brother was eight years old when he started saving money from mowing lawns. Quietly. Carefully. He didn't tell anyone. Not me. Not our sisters. Not our parents. He folded dollar bills under his mattress and tucked coins into the lining of an old backpack. With every delivery, he was building an escape—one envelope, one tip, one mile at a time.

We all wanted out in their own ways. But he was the first to *act*.

We lived in a house that lacked warmth and stability. Fear soaked it, and it trembled under our father's rage. The rules changed with his mood, and punishment came without warning. My brother, older than me, had already endured years of it. Switches are the topic of discussion. The absence of sound. The shame. I remember watching him nights, staring out the window like he could will himself away—his face hard, his jaw clenched, as if he were daring the stars to carry him someplace else.

And then, one day, he did it.

No warning. No goodbye. Just… gone.

He snuck out in the early hours, before sunrise, with his bag of clothes and cash. I don't know how he got to the station I guess he hitchhiked. I don't even know how he knew *where* to go. But he boarded a Greyhound bus headed for Ohio—a place where he knew the police officer and his wife lived, and maybe, just maybe, a sliver of hope.

He was eight.

That kind of courage? It's not built on adventure. It's built on desperation.

I like to imagine him sitting by the window, watching the landscape shift, heart pounding in his chest. Alone. But free. At least for a little while. I wonder what he thought about. Was it what he'd say when he got there? Was it the fear of being caught? Or was it just the quiet hum of possibility, of breathing for once without the air tasting like dread?

He made it.

He made it to Ohio.

But not for long.

Our father found out. I don't know whether someone recognized him. Or if someone made a phone call. But somehow, something interrupted our freedom. The world always seemed to loop back to him.

My dad went to get him, and all hell broke loose.

And when he walked through the front door, he didn't return to hugs or relief. There was no "We're glad you're safe." No "Tell us what happened." No questions. Just punishment.

Serious punishment.

The kind that didn't show up as bruises, but as control. Dad searched through his belongings. His independence disappeared. His grounding resulted in isolation. Not just from the outside world, but from *himself.* And perhaps worst of all, someone forbade him from *even running away.*

But I knew something they didn't.

That trip? It changed him.

It wasn't just a bus ride. It was a declaration. A glimpse of a potential life. *El*sewhere, he tasted the air. He watched strangers smile at each other, unafraid. He felt in his bones that something better existed beyond the walls confining us.

And you can't take that back.

That fire doesn't go out.

Over the years, my brother carried the same fire. It fueled him through more pain, more chaos. It reminded him that there was more to life than the screaming, the secrets, and the silent dinners. That even though he came back to the same house, he wasn't the same boy.

The next time he ran away—years later—it would be different. That time, he didn't come back.

But at eight, with a bus ticket and a lawn mowing worth of dreams, he proved something I never forgot.

That escape is possible.

That bravery doesn't always look like standing tall—it sometimes looks like a boy sitting alone on a bus, heading toward a sliver of light.

And that no matter how far we're dragged back, the dream of freedom survives.

He had it once, and he never let it go.

Chapter 34

Promises in the Dust

Broken...

The promise sounded like salvation.

My father told my grandparents—his own parents—that Texas would be different. That things were changing. That if they came down, he'd build them a home. Not just a place to stay, but a proper home. With a porch. A garden. Maybe even peace. After years of living with regret and ghosts, they believed him.

They packed up everything they had in Ohio—old photo albums, kitchenware, a rocking chair that had survived three generations—and moved south. The air was fresh in Texas, hotter and heavy with dreams. For two years, they lived with us, hoping for the house's completion, fulfilling promises, and a life finally destined for them.

But the foundation never came.

The blueprints were a lie.

There was no house.

And while they waited, they watched.

They saw the truth unravel within the walls we called home. Yelling is occurring. The control. The way my mom shrank in the presence of their son. How the kids became shadows, quiet and obedient, flinching when footsteps approached. They witnessed bruises—not always on skin, but in spirit. They saw how the light inside each of us dimmed a little more each week.

And they did nothing out of fear.

They said nothing out of fear.

Their silence? It screamed.

As the years passed, and no home appeared, my grandparents saw the truth. The lies weren't just occasional. They were constant. Nothing was ever going to be built—not a house, not a future, not trust.

My grandmother, who once crocheted baby blankets and smiled with her entire face, stopped smiling.

My grandfather, who used to whistle in the mornings, just sat on the porch in silence.

Two years.

That's how long they waited.

Two years of empty promises. Of watching from the outside in. Of seeing the damage built like dust on unwashed windows.

Then one day, they left.

No dramatic farewell. No confrontation. Just bags packed. A quiet drive north. And Ohio, waiting with familiar roads and old regrets.

They went back to the place they once thought they'd escaped.

They never looked back.

And in a way, I don't blame them. They lacked the knowledge to repair the damage. But what still stings, even now, is the fact that they *could* have tried. They could have stepped in. Asked questions. Offered safety. Given us a lifeline.

But they folded into the lie. They kept their heads down. And they left us behind.

I sometimes wonder if they talk about it. If they ever told anyone back in Ohio what really happened during those two years in Texas. Or if they buried it like everything else.

But I remember.

I remember the promise that turned to dust.

I remember waiting for a home that was never built.

And I remember watching my grandparents drive away, not just from a house, but from *us*.

From the truth.

Chapter 35

The Echo of Two Traumas

Haunted...

It was early—too early for the sun to feel like comfort—when my sister slipped through the front door, clutching her music folder and trying not to wake anyone. Thirteen and determined, she'd recently earned a spot in her school choir. That morning was supposed to be special. She had a solo. She wore her best blouse, ironed the night before, and combed her long hair straight. Our house still slept in shadows when she stepped into the quiet cold.

But she never made it to choir.

Three boys waited at the park near the school we barely knew, older boys with something cruel in their silence. They didn't speak. They didn't have to. She didn't even scream until after it started. Her solo for the day was a cry fractured by fear. They knocked her into the dirt, and one of them grabbed her wrist and twisted until something snapped. Her left arm hung limp like a broken wing. Her face slammed into the grass, skin tearing against the gravel. They scattered after they had done their damage, like boys who thought no one would believe her anyway.

She stumbled to school with one swollen eye shut, with blood matting her hair and shirt. She said nothing. Not at first. Trembling on the floor and whispering, "I did nothing wrong," over and over, she sat in the bathroom for an hour before the principal found her. They called my mom, and the police came. They took a statement, and off she went to the hospital. We never saw the consequences. Only more silence.

The attack didn't happen in isolation. It ripped open another wound.

After that day, she never walked alone again. She stopped singing, too. And sometimes, even years later, she would wake up screaming, her arm cradled like it still ached, whispering words she'd never explain.

Two traumas. One body. And a mind trying to grow in soil turned to ash.

Sometimes my sister's eyes carried two moments: one bright blue, the other dark and unchanging.

What happened to my sister at thirteen proved
what I had feared all along—abuse didn't just live
inside our home; it roamed the neighborhood,
lurking behind ordinary doors, waiting for its
chance to strike *twice*.

Chapter 36

Across The Street To the Left

Detour...

She never walked down the street with a stroller.

That's the image I used to hold onto—my sister pushing her baby in the sunshine, waving to neighbors, her life maybe not perfect, but steady. Safe. But that dream never came true. The house across the street on the left stole it.

It started slowly, like all things that break. She was thirteen when things really began to shift. She was already hurting long before that—kidnapped at seven, terrified in her own home, growing up in a house where yelling was normal and silence was survival. But thirteen was when the crack in her life split wide open.

That's when she was attacked.

From that point on, her eyes changed. Her spirit dimmed. She started sneaking out at night, slipping through the back door when the rest of us pretended to be asleep. I don't know where she went every time, but I knew she wasn't coming back whole.

That's when she started going over to the house across the street on the left.

He lived there. Same age, slick, dangerous in that way broken girls sometimes confuse with love. At first it seemed innocent—just talking, just hanging out. But it changed fast. She was spending nights there. Then days. Then everything.

She started using drugs. Not the kind you experiment with for fun. The kind you take to numb out the world. To forget. To disappear.

She got pregnant not long after. She was just a kid herself, but already her life had splintered into something she couldn't fix.

Our mother screamed when she found out. Threw things. Cried. But my sister didn't cry. She just stared past us, numb, like she'd been expecting this kind of fallout all along. "I'm keeping the baby," she said. And there was no room for discussion.

She didn't stay at our house after that. She moved in with him—the one from the house on the left across the street. He wasn't much older than her, but he had the power. The control. He told her what to do, where to go, to whom she could talk. He convinced her this was love. But it wasn't love. It was just another prison.

I remember watching her walk down the street one last time. No suitcase, no backpack—just a plastic bag in one hand and her future in the other. She didn't say goodbye. She didn't look back. Just disappeared into that house like the door had been waiting for her.

She never came home again.

We heard bits and pieces. That she dropped out of school. That they fought all the time. That she was still using. She did not see a doctor during the pregnancy. That she was alone.

Then came the call.

She was in labor. Something was wrong. She'd waited too long to go to the hospital. The pain wasn't just contractions—it was her appendix. It had burst. She was septic. Sixteen and my sister was dying.

The doctors rushed her into surgery. The baby had to come out immediately. She was cut open before they even knew if she'd survive. They tried to clean out the infection, tried to save what they could. She hovered between life and death while the child she hadn't even held yet was crying in the next room.

We sat in the waiting room, stunned. Numb. Frozen in that familiar way trauma makes you forget how to breathe.

She survived.

Barely.

When she woke up, pale and stitched and hollow, the first thing she said wasn't "Am I okay?" or "What happened?" It was, "Where's my baby?"

That was the only moment she showed a flicker of the girl we used to know. Just for a second. Then it was gone again.

The weeks after were a blur. Recovery. A baby to care for. A life she wasn't ready for—but had no choice but to live.

She didn't come back home. She stayed with him. In that same house. The house on the left across the street. The house that had become her world. Her cage.

She never walked down the street with a stroller. Never had the peaceful moment of being a young mom out in the sunshine with a cooing baby and a hopeful future. That wasn't her story. Instead, her days were filled with chaos, pain, and trying to hold herself together while everything else fell apart.

And the truth is—no one saved her. Not then.

The house on the left became the place where the final pieces of her innocence was taken. It wasn't just a location. It was a symbol of everything that failed her—our broken home, the predators outside of it, the silence of adults who looked the other way.

I never walk past that house anymore

But I bet it looks the same. Shutters still chipped. Porch still creaking. I now recognize it as more than a house; it was a place where significant changes occurred for a girl who had different expectations.

That house never once got the blame it deserved.

But I remember. And I won't forget.

Chapter 37

The Paper Route

Independence...

There was no sleeping in at our house. Not even on Sundays.

Especially not on Sundays.

Long before sunrise, while the world slept, we roused ourselves. Pulling on layers over our pajamas. Lacing up worn-out shoes. Rubbing the sleep out of our eyes with frozen fingers. Sunday morning meant one thing: the paper route.

It wasn't just one of us—it was all of us. Every sibling. Every small pair of feet. Ink-stained fingers and early morning footsteps on cold pavement built our childhood. The paper was thick on Sundays, filled with glossy advertisements and colorful circulars. Heavy enough to break your back when the stack was high. Heavy enough to remind you that you didn't really get to be a kid.

We started before we even understood what money really was. Before we could comprehend what "earning" meant or that we wouldn't get to keep what we worked for. Dad said it was good for us—said it would teach us discipline, that it would build character. What it really taught us was that sleep was a luxury we couldn't afford, and neither was freedom.

We'd drag heavy canvas bags down the streets, our breath visible in the frigid air, our arms aching before we even reached the second block. Sometimes the papers would be late, and we'd sit on the curb in the dark, waiting for the delivery truck like it was the most natural thing in the world. No complaints. No questions. Just a tired silence.

We knew there was no getting out of it.

Our friends went to birthday parties. They joined sports teams. They had sleepovers on Saturday nights. We didn't. Saturday nights were for bundling papers, for rubber bands and folding, for stuffing ads and getting everything ready for the 2:00 a.m. grind. There was no staying up late. There was no sleeping in.

And even if we tried to resist, we couldn't.

Dad made it clear: this was our job. This was our duty. This was what we owed the family. And when payday came around, he was the one waiting by the door. Not with pride or gratitude—but with an open hand. We worked. He collected. Week after week, we handed over our envelopes without a word.

He took all.

Not some. Not most. All.

He told us it was for bills. For food. For the family. But somehow, we still lived in the same crumbling house. Still wore hand-me-downs and went to school hungry. Still wondered why the lights got turned off some months, or why the cupboards were empty while he always had cigarettes and beer.

We never saw that money again.

It didn't go toward clothes for school or bikes or anything a kid might dream of buying. It went into the black hole of his control. He kept us busy, broke, and tired enough that we didn't have the energy to rebel.

And maybe that was the point.

Maybe the paper route wasn't just about money. Maybe it was about keeping us in line. Keeps us from asking too many questions. The paper route ensured our exhaustion, preventing us from noticing what was really happening at home.

It wasn't normal. But it was all we knew.

On holiday, we still delivered. In snow, in ice, in rain that soaked through every layer we had. I remember the way the papers would get soggy in the cold, how our fingers would go numb from stuffing them into mailboxes. No gloves thick enough. No jacket is warm enough.

We kept walking.

Because he said we had to.

Because there was no choice.

Even when we were sick, even when we cried, it didn't matter. The papers had to go out. His word was law. And we were just the kids caught beneath it.

Sometimes I wonder if any of the people on those routes ever thought about the children who delivered their papers. If they ever saw our tired eyes or noticed how small we were to be hauling such heavy loads. If they ever thought to tip us or say thank you.

Some did occasionally. A warm smile. Someone folded a dollar into a Christmas card. But mostly, we were invisible. Ghosts in the morning fog.

Shadows moved across their lawns before the sun came up.

Years later, when other kids talked about their childhood memories—cartoons, cereal, family trips—I thought about ink smudges and sore backs and the sound of our dad's voice barking at us to "hustle." I thought about payday being something we dreaded because it meant handing over every cent to a man who never said thank you.

It took a long time to understand how wrong it was.

How what should have been a lesson in responsibility became another tool of control. Another way to steal our time. Our effort. Our innocence.

It wasn't about helping the family. It was about power.

And even now, when I see a paper tossed on a porch, part of me flinches. My hands remember the cold. My legs remember the weight. And my heart remembers the ache of knowing I was working hard—but never for myself.

We didn't have a childhood.

Chapter 38

The Words That Weren't Mine

Silenced...

I was young when I wrote my first piece. Not just schoolwork or scribbles in the margins of a notebook—but something real, something that felt like it came from deep inside me. It was just a few lines, a small poem, really, but it felt big to me. Important.

Through rain, hail, sleet, or snow,
The Press is on the go

It came to me in a flash, like a spark lighting something within. I wrote it out on lined paper with the care that only children give to their first treasures. Again and again, I remember reading it aloud to myself, letting the rhythm sink into my chest. I felt proud—more than that; I felt *seen.* Like maybe finally, I'd found something that was mine in a house where very little ever belonged to me.

I showed it to my dad.

And for a moment, I saw something I rarely saw on his face: interest. My dad said nothing. He looked at the words as if they meant something. I thought maybe this was it—maybe this was the moment where he'd say, "I'm proud of you."

Instead, a few days later, he showed me the local paper.

My poem was in it.

But my name was not.

They printed his name beneath it — bold, clean, and official. As if he had written it. As if those words—my words—had come from *him.*

I stared at the page in disbelief. I remember how my face flushed hot, how my heart sank into my stomach. He stood behind me, arms crossed. Proud of *himself.*

When I spoke up—when I told him, "I wrote that"—he didn't deny it. But he didn't apologize either. He looked me dead in the eye and said, "You're just a little person. No one would believe you wrote that."

It crushed something inside me.

He wasn't just taking my words—he was taking my *voice*. My worth. My confidence. In one sentence, he reduced me to nothing. A whisper. And when your own father tells you that your truth doesn't matter, you believe him.

I refrained from fighting. I remained silent. Having: Folding the newspaper, tucking it away, I carried the silence with me like a hidden bruise.

My mother and siblings knew the truth. My reading of it came to their minds. They remembered how excited I'd been. They told me it wasn't fair. But their comfort couldn't undo the damage.

After that, I hid my writing.

I still wrote, of course. I *had* to. It was like breathing. Late at night, when the house was quiet, I'd scribble poems and stories in spiral notebooks and shove them under my mattress like contraband. I was afraid—not just of someone stealing my words again, but of someone *seeing* them.

When I was older, I lent my voice out again.

A friend—someone I trusted—asked me to write her a poem. It was for a school project, something fun. She wanted it to be about the Muppets. I agreed, feeling nervous but excited. It took a lot of effort. I made it clever and sweet. I wanted it to reflect her request, but also my own creative touch.

When I gave it to her, I said only one thing:

"Please, just include my name on it."

She promised she would.

I waited eagerly, hoping maybe this time would be different. That maybe my words would finally be mine publicly. But on the day of submission, the teacher read it aloud in class and only attributed it to her. My name was nowhere to be found.

She stood there smiling, basking in the praise from the teacher and classmates, nodding as if every word belonged to her.

And once again, I felt that familiar sting.

That hollow ache in the chest. Disconnecting from my voice bitterly reminded me that people loved it.

I confronted her after class. Asked why? She laughed it off. Said it was just a joke. Said it didn't matter. That no one cared who wrote it.

But *I* cared.

Because those words were mine.

And for the second time in my life, someone taught me that my creations were only valuable if someone else claimed them. Being quiet and creative made me easy to take form. That the world didn't see little girls from broken homes as poets or writers. Just as tools.

So, I stopped again.

Years passed. I wrote in private. I rarely shared. Even when people complimented me on something I said or wrote, I deflected. I had learned that visibility came with risk—and I had risked enough.

But even as I tried to ignore it, the words still lived in me. Clawing at my ribs, they reached inside. They whispered to me in quiet moments. They begged to come out—not for credit, not for applause—but just to *be*.

Because writing, for me, was never just about being good at something. It was about surviving. About making sense of a world that constantly tried to erase me. About claiming space in a life where others never freely gave it.

Now I see it for what it was.

My father took my first poem because he wanted
to be admired—because he saw something
beautiful in it and needed that beauty to reflect
on *him*. My friend took my Muppet poem, unaware
of how sharing it affected me.

Neither of them understood what it meant to steal a
voice.

But I do.

And I've spent a lifetime reclaiming it.

Word by word. Page by page. Even now, with the
ghosts of those moments still lingering, I write.

I wrote that poem.
I wrote them *both*.
And I've written every word since.

And now I write with my name on it.

Because I am not just a little person.
I am a writer.
And I am not hiding anymore.

Chapter 39

Her Horse, Her Haven

Sanctuary...

My sister and I are just a year apart — close in age, close in childhood, and close in the way only siblings who've weathered the same storm can be. But even in that closeness, there were things I couldn't give her, wounds I couldn't heal, and moments where all I could do was watch as she tried to stitch herself back together with whatever scraps of peace she could find.

For her, that peace came as a horse.

Not a show horse, she wasn't from a fancy stable or bred for ribbons. She didn't have papers or a pedigree. But to her, she was everything. She was strength. Silent, she was. She had a soft muzzle pressing into her shoulder on the days she couldn't speak. A steady heartbeat when everything else in our lives fell off rhythm.

She was hers.

When the world inside our house spun too fast—
when Dad's words cut deeper than belts ever
could, and the air felt thick with things unsaid—
she would go to her. Sometimes without a word.
Sometimes without shoes. Just the screen door
creaking shut behind her and her figure
disappearing down the sidewalk to the pasture like
a shadow chasing its light.

And she was always there.

Waiting.

Questions were unasked by her. There was no
judgment of her. She didn't talk over her or
demand she smile. Standing patiently, she allowed
her to run her hands through her hair, bury her face
in her neck, and breathe in the earthy smell of
safety. She knew when she needed stillness. She
knew when she needed motion. Sometimes she'd
just sit with her in the stall, legs pulled up to her
chest, resting her head against her warm side.
Other times, she'd saddle her and ride hard and
fast, letting the wind whip through her hair like it
could strip away the fear.

She was more than an animal. She was an escape.

She told me once, in a whisper, that when she was
with her, she didn't feel like a burden. Didn't feel
broken or small. She just *was*. Fully and freely

herself. No fear of judgment. No tightrope to walk. She and her horse moved together, as if made from the same dust and dreams.

She saved her in ways none of us could.

She gave her a reason to get up some mornings. A reason to believe not everything in this world would hurt her. And maybe most importantly, she gave her control. In a life largely dictated by others' anger, caring for something kind empowered her. She brushed her, fed her, talked to her like a friend. She never answered, but she swore she understood.

And I believe in her.

When I watched them together, I saw something different in her. Not the scared girl who flinched when the door slammed. Not the teenager holding back tears at dinner. I saw someone lighter. Softer. Smiling without fear of what might come next. *She needed that.*

We all did, in our own way. But the horse was hers. Her sacred space. She was calm within the storm.

And as we grew older and life pulled us in different directions, I never forgot the way she looked when she was with her—free, whole, unshattered.

The world attempted to deprive us of many things. But it couldn't take her horse.

Chapter 40

The Day She Finally Did It

Breakthrough...

It was the moment we had waited for without even knowing how long we'd been holding our breath. The day my mother finally said the words aloud. The day she finally broke free.

"I'm divorcing him."

There were no fireworks included. It didn't happen in a courtroom or in front of a crowd. She said it in a quiet, maybe even trembling voice. But for us—for all of us kids—those words were louder than any scream. Those words shattered our foundation. They were words I thought I might never hear. But she said them. And everything changed.

I was fourteen.

Just old enough to know what it all meant. Old enough to feel the weight of what had come before and what we hoped might come next. Old enough to understand that, finally, they couldn't take me away. Not this time. Now that I had a voice, the system would hear. I was no longer just a small child shuffled from house to house, wondering if the people I loved would disappear again. I was no longer in danger of being put back in foster care.

And I wasn't alone.

My brother, my sisters had all been waiting, aching, wishing for something to give. We had watched my mother bend, break, and rebuild herself repeatedly, all under the crushing weight of a man who never loved her the way she deserved. A man who controlled, manipulated, gaslit, and emotionally tortured her day in and day out.

There were no bruises. But the damage? It was everywhere.

Her flinching at raised voices showed. The way she reacted to raised voices was revealing. In the way she apologized for taking up space. Her eyes always scanned the room, calculating what mood he might be in before speaking. It was a life lived on tiptoe. A house that breathed tension and silence like oxygen. A home where joy walked quietly in but rarely stayed.

Despite that, she stayed. For years.

She stayed because she thought it was right. Because she thought it was what God wanted. She thought she couldn't survive on her own. But mostly, she stayed because she was afraid that if she left—*they* would come for us again. The situation. The system needs to be updated. Those who thought they were doing right by separating families never saw the heartbreak it caused.

She had lived that nightmare before—watching her babies taken, split apart like pieces of a puzzle never meant to be scattered. Two to relatives. Two to strangers. That fear haunted her. So, she stayed.

But we saw her break. Slowly. Quietly. A little more each year.

And then something shifted.

I don't know if it was something he said. Something she saw. Or maybe just a moment of stillness when she realized she was worth more. Maybe she looked at us—older now, tougher, worn—but still standing. Still hoping. And she decided we had suffered enough.

She was done.

When she told us, we all looked at her as if she had grown wings. Like we were seeing her for the first time. There were tears, of course. Not of sorrow— but of *release*. We didn't cry because we were afraid. We cried because it was finally over.

The shouting. The threats. Manipulation that was happening. The constant walking on eggshells. The fear that came with every turn of the doorknob, every creak in the floorboards when he came home angry.

Gone.

He wasn't gone yet, not physically. But the power he held? That was slipping. And we could feel it.

It was the first time in my life that I remember feeling *relief* as something physical. My shoulders lowered. I took a deep breath. My body relaxed in ways I hadn't known it could. It was like I'd been holding a scream inside me for years—and now I could breathe.

We didn't have a parade. We didn't celebrate with cake. But we celebrated *quietly*. With peace. The stillness was so profound it brought tears to your eyes, a feeling both alien and strangely fitting.

And my mother… she changed.

Bit by bit. Day by day. She started coming back to us. Her voice grew stronger. Her laughter returned—soft at first, then fuller, more certain. She smiled more. When she spoke, she looked us in the eye. She stopped apologizing for things that weren't her fault. She stood taller.

She still carried her scars. We all did. But now, she carried them with pride. Like proof she had survived. That she had clawed her way out of the darkness and brought her children with her.

People asked how we did it.

How she did it.

How someone with no money, no formal education past eighth grade, no support system to lean on, could find the strength to walk away.

They didn't see what we saw.

They didn't see the nights she stayed up praying. In the mornings she got up before the sun went to work so we could eat. The way she bit her tongue to keep the peace, endured insults to protect us, and poured every ounce of her spirit into keeping our family alive.

They didn't see the fire in her—the fire he had tried to put out a thousand times and failed.

They didn't see the woman who had raised warriors.

She didn't just divorce him. She divorced the fear. The silence. Someone forced her into that life through manipulation and control.

She just didn't set herself free. She set *us* free.

And that's why, even all these years later, I
remember that moment not with sadness, but with
deep and overwhelming *gratitude.*

Because the day she finally did it—
Was the day we got our mother back.
And the day we realized nothing had ever truly
broken us.
Just waiting to be made whole.

Chapter 41

The White Bread

Liberation...

After the divorce, everything in our lives shifted—quietly at first, like the way dusk falls before you notice the night. The house still looked the same on the outside, and our school routines didn't change overnight. But inside, where it mattered most, the atmosphere was unmistakably different. It was in the way we woke up with a little less weight on our chests, and it was especially in the way we went grocery shopping that first Saturday.

We were with Mom. Just us and her. There was no pressure, no barking commands, no storm waiting to be unleashed over a misplaced receipt or a forgotten item. We moved through the grocery store like a group of explorers walking freely for the first time on undiscovered land. The fluorescent lights felt brighter, almost friendly. And there, in aisle five, we did something we'd never done before—we reached for a loaf of soft, fluffy white bread.

For us, that bread represented a significant change. We were not allowed to have it before because our father considered it unhealthy. He referred to it as "fluff bread" and believed that real bread should be dark, grainy, and thick enough to sink in soup. Consequently, we ate dense whole wheat bread that turned stale quickly and left crumbs in your throat. As for jelly, grape was the only option available, and there were no exceptions. Alternative flavors like strawberry, raspberry, or peach were not considered. Asking for different options was viewed unfavorably.

We held a loaf of white bread that felt like cotton. We quietly laughed, feeling like we were getting away with something. Mom smiled - tired but genuine. She didn't say no or flinch. It was just bread, but it meant much more.

That afternoon, we sat at the kitchen table and made sandwiches with white bread, ham, cheese, mayo, and strawberry jelly. We tried various kinds of jelly, treating them like trophies, and giggled as we tasted them, feeling like we were biting into forbidden fruit.

Fridays were designated for cleaning out the fridge in our kitchen. This involved following Dad's system, which combined all leftovers, such as baked chicken from Monday or boiled cabbage from Tuesday, into a pot. He called it stew and would add flour to thicken the mixture without measuring. The mixture would bubble and pop in the pot before being served in bowls. We ate it spoonful by spoonful, occasionally wiping our tongues with napkins when he wasn't looking. He never ate the stew himself; instead, he prepared a separate plate with items like fried eggs and sausage or a sandwich.

So, when the divorce became real—when the slamming doors were gone, and the threats became memories instead of daily thunderclaps—we started throwing away the leftovers. Not because we were wasteful, but because we finally had a choice. If we didn't like it, we didn't have to eat it. We weren't scared anymore. There was no looming figure with clenched teeth and cold eyes forcing us to prove our gratitude through suffering. That alone made the kitchen feel warmer.

I remember the first time Mom cleaned the fridge post-divorce. She pulled out a container of leftover spaghetti. It was only two days old, but she turned and asked gently, "Anyone want this again?" None of us did. She nodded and tossed it. Just like that. And nothing bad happened. No yelling. No lecture about starving children. No accusations of laziness or entitlement. Just a clean shelf and the freedom to decide.

We bought snacks we'd always wanted: fruit snacks, string cheese, Gatorade, orange juice, and Little Debbie snacks. We stocked our cabinets openly and didn't need to hide the wrappers.

It's amazing how food can be symbolic. That loaf of white bread wasn't just sandwich material; it represented our new, safer home where choices were respected, and joy was free.

There were difficult days. The absence of a parent does not always feel like relief. Sometimes it is noticeable. Sometimes it is perplexing. However, the moments spent around the kitchen table— laughing with jelly on our cheeks and breadcrumbs on our plates—marked the start of our recovery.

And to this day, I still smile when I buy a loaf of white bread. It may not be the healthiest choice, but to me, it tastes like freedom.

Your stomach is full.

Chapter 42

Across the Street, But Never Gone

Lingering...

We thought he was gone.

After everything — after the court papers and the shouting and the finality of the divorce, we thought we were finally free. We had tasted that sweet, delicate thing called peace. Sleep had overtaken us once again. We started leaving the bathroom door open while brushing our teeth and stopped flinching when someone raised their voice. Slowly, we let ourselves breathe.

But he wasn't gone. He had just crossed the street.

Literally.

He rented a room directly across from the house. Not a different town. Not a different block. Just steps away—close enough that we could see his front door from our front porch. Close enough that we could feel his presence even when he wasn't looking our way. The close that turned every open window into a vulnerability. Every walk down the driveway into an act of defiance.

He never really left us alone. He just changed tactics.

What kind of man moves across the street from the family he terrorized? From the wife who finally escaped him and the children who watched from behind bedroom doors as the yelling turned to threats, as the house filled with tension like smoke? What kind of man stays close not because he cares—but because he *wants them to know* they're never free?

He still watched us.

From his front stoop, from his parked car, from behind his curtains. We'd see the flick of a blind, the glint of his cigarette, the slow pacing of his feet across the gravel. There was no telling what he was thinking, what he might do. That was the worst part. The not knowing. Walking on eggshells even after we'd swept the house clean of him.

It was a haunting—except the ghost had skin and bone and a key to the past.

And then one day, he came back.

He walked into the house as if he owned it. Like he had never left. The ink on the divorce papers felt insignificant. I don't recall how he got inside—

whether he unlocked the door or broke it down. All I remember is the look in his eyes.

Dead.

Empty.

Unhinged.

He wasn't just angry—he was *gone.*

And in his hand was a pistol.

Time stopped. My breath froze in my chest. I remember the look—not just from him, but from our mother, from my siblings, from me. A flurry of panic and motion that didn't happen. We backed up, and just stood still, too paralyzed by fear.

And he stood there, arm raised, pistol clenched. Eyes wild. Mouth moving fast with words I can't even remember. Threats. Promises. Desperation. Maybe all three.

It wasn't the first time he'd threatened us.

But this time felt different.

This time he looked like he *meant it.*

And just like that, the safe space we had finally rebuilt shattered. The floor beneath us cracked open again, and we were right back in. Back in the house where fear ruled, where nothing was ours, not even our own safety.

I remember praying. Not to be saved—but for him just to walk out. Departing. To spare my mom. To save us. So, we may live; Living to see another day is our goal. I don't remember whether the police were called but I do know he left on his own.

Again.

That should've been the end.

But it wasn't.

He didn't get arrested, and they didn't take him away. He just left.

Safety isn't just about locks and laws. Safety is the ability to sleep at night without checking the windows. It's being able to walk down your street without wondering who's watching. It's living without the shadow of a man who once said he'd end your life standing three steps from your front door.

He might have lived across the street. But what he really did was *loom*.

He loomed over us in every creak of the floorboard, in every knock at the door. He loomed in our dreams. We saw exhaustion in our mother's eyes. In the way we double-checked behind us when we walked home from school.

I hated that house after that.

Not because of its size or its shape—but because of the proximity. Because every time I looked out the window, I had to see *him*. And every time I saw him; I remembered that moment. The handgun. The chaos. From someone who helped bring me into the world comes the threat of being erased.

Eventually, he moved away. Or maybe someone forced him to. I don't remember how or why. I just know that one day, he wasn't there anymore.

And still—it took years to stop expecting him to come back. Because when trauma lives across the street, you never stop looking at the door.

Chapter 43

Eve

Unease...

Her name was Eve.

She came into our lives like a storm that never touched down—visible from a distance, unsettling, but at first, untouchable. She was our father's new wife. The woman he married not long after the divorce, like he couldn't stand to be alone for even a breath.

He moved on fast. No grieving, no reflection. No attempt to reconcile what he'd done to us or our mother. Just a clean break—for him. For us, the pieces still lay scattered.

And then came the house.

Not for us. Not for the kids he had left behind in a crumbling neighborhood or the wife who had clawed her way through survival every single day. No, the new house was for *her*. For Eve. It was in a better part of town. It was a brand-new home, complete with trimmed hedges, clean floors, and new appliances. It was a peaceful home, without raised voices. It had never been cursed with the shadows of our childhood.

To witness him provide a residence to another individual, one which we had earnestly requested. What we had thought maybe, just maybe, we were going to get after the divorce. But he didn't look back. He walked into his new life as if we were ghosts from another time. As if the years he spent breaking us down weren't even worth remembering.

He gave Eve comfort, calm, and attention—at least in the beginning. But he had given us only fear.

He saw our predicament from across town. He knew our mother was barely getting by. He knew we were still living in the same neighborhood we'd nearly died in—literally. The same street where his violence had unfolded like a storm behind closed doors. Despite that, he offered nothing. No help. No remorse. Not even a phone call.

It was as if we had never existed.

And Eve... She became a symbol to us. Not really a person, not even a villain, just *proof.* Proof that he had always been capable of being better. Of showing kindness. Of keeping his hands to himself and his anger in check. He just chose not to—with us.

I often wondered what she thought. If she looked into his eyes and saw anything real. If she noticed how tightly he gripped things. How quickly could his voice turn. If she ever saw a flicker of something cruel when he didn't get his way.

Because we had.

We'd lived it.

She got a version of him none of us recognized— at first. He wore charm like a second skin. Smiled at all the right times. Played the part. But people like him can wear a mask only for so long. The truth always finds its way out.

And it did.

The marriage didn't last.

Soon enough, Eve saw what we saw. Similar fury. The same control. The same manipulation just polished a bit differently. It didn't take her long. Maybe months. Maybe a year. But then the truth became too big to ignore.

He lost her love. He lost the lie he was trying to live inside.

The divorce came quickly.

And when it did, there was no sympathy from us. No surprise either. Only the bitter satisfaction of knowing someone else saw the monster we knew too well. He had fooled her briefly. But monsters don't change. They just move.

And yet—even knowing her marriage ended the same way our mothers did, it didn't erase what he had done to us. It didn't undo the fact that he had walked away from his own children without a second thought, only to recreate himself with someone new.

When it fell apart, we didn't rush to comfort him. We weren't interested in his heartbreak. He'd already caused too much of ours. We didn't pity him. We didn't hate Eve either. If anything, we pitied her. She had walked into something none of us would ever wish on another woman.

She left, and she never looked back.

He was alone again.

Back in a rental, back to pacing and yelling at the walls, back to the isolation he had created. Only now there was no wife making excuses for him. No kids he could control. No house, no charade, no peace.

Just the wreckage.

And maybe that's the justice the world gave us—small, late, and far from enough — it was something. Watching the house, he built fall apart felt like a strange closure. Not joy. Not revenge. Just a chapter closed.

We were still poor. Still struggling. Still healing.

But at least we weren't living a lie.

Our mother never got that house. Never got the tranquil life. But she got her dignity. She got us. And in the end, that counted for more than any mortgage or freshly painted walls. She stood tall when everything around her collapsed. She raised us through storms he started and never helped clean up.

And we? We endured.

We learned to build safety in other ways. During hushed discussions. In locks on the doors. In the memories we rewrote with each passing year. We weren't just the kids he left behind.

We were survivors.

And when I think of Eve now, I don't think of her as the woman who replaced our mother. I think of her as a reminder that truth always finds a way through.

Even when it hides behind white fences and welcome mats.

Chapter 44

The Second Escape

Flight...

The first time my brother left, it felt like abandonment.

He was just a boy when he ran. Not running away from us, but from the chaos, the pain, and the home that doesn't feel like a home at all. Fear had swallowed him and chewed him up in the system, spit him back out into a world that didn't know what to do with kids like us. That first escape was raw, desperate, and terrifying.

But the second time?

That was different.

That time, when he packed his things and left, it wasn't out of desperation. Hope was present. It was strength. It was *freedom.*

He was older then—tired, yes, and maybe a little bruised by the past, but wiser. There was no screaming fight. No dramatic storming out. Just a quiet goodbye, a small bag, and a promise he'd keep in his own way: that this time, he wasn't leaving to disappear.

He was leaving to become.

My brother moved in with friends—good people, kind people—who needed help with their kids. And in helping them, something shifted in him. Perhaps the surrounding, unforced laughter may have been the reason. Maybe it was the stability of a home that didn't echo with threats. Maybe it was just being seen, finally, as someone *good*, capable, and dependable.

He found himself by giving to others.

He drove every day from Azle to our school. Long Texas miles through morning fog and afternoon heat. Silence enveloped him. He didn't boast. Day after day, he quietly showed up and did what was necessary. He worked, helped with homework, and kept things running. In a world that had rarely worked for him, he became the one people could count on.

And in that consistency, he grew.

You could see it in his posture. In the calmness in his eyes. In the way his laugh changed—not the sarcastic one we all learned to mask pain, but a deeper, fuller laugh, like he'd finally heard something genuinely funny after years of noise.

Dad was no longer in control.

That's what changed everything.

This wasn't like before, when every decision we made had to pass through a filter of fear. When our lives bent and buckled around his moods. This time, Dad couldn't touch him. Not physically, not mentally, not emotionally. My brother set a boundary and crossed it—into a life where a man who never treated him like a son no longer dictated his worth.

He became his own person. Not the boy Dad tried to break. Not the ghost drifting from couch to couch. He was working, helping, *living*.

And he started dreaming again.

It began in small ways. Ideas he'd toss around in the kitchen. Conversations about the future. Plans, even. He talked about getting a better job, maybe going to school. About one day having a family of his own—and doing everything differently. We'd sit on the porch and talk, and I'd look at him like I was seeing someone I hadn't known in years.

He hadn't left *us*.
He had finally left *him*.

There's something sacred about watching someone rebuild themselves from the ashes of a childhood they didn't choose. My brother didn't just survive—he remade himself, piece by piece. And he did it without fanfare. With no one handing him a blueprint. Just the knowing that the past would not win.

He still came to see us.

He wasn't gone in a way that hurt. He was present. Reliable. He checked on Mom. Helped with little things around the house. Showed up when things got hard. But there was something different now in the way he stood, the way he moved in a room. He wasn't shrinking anymore.

He was *becoming*.

And for the first time, I felt something I hadn't felt in a long time when I thought of him *peace*.

We had always been close, my brother and me. Trauma had a way of tying knots between us, ones that held through even the worst of storms. But seeing him find his footing—that was something else. It made me believe maybe we could all get there. Maybe healing wasn't a myth. Maybe we could claw our way into something better, too.

He led the way.

I don't think he knows how much that meant to me. His miles driven, hours worked and acts of love given to a family in need proved that we wouldn't become like our father. That love, when chosen freely and given gently, was stronger than any scar.

The second escape wasn't an escape at all.
It was a *return*—to himself.

I watched him reclaim his voice. Take ownership of his story. Refuse to be defined by what he had endured. And I realized something simple but life-changing:

Sometimes leaving isn't running away.
Sometimes, you actively pursue your destined self.

Chapter 45

The Bridegroom of Betrayal

Heartbreak...

Some men build legacies. Others leave wreckage.
My father—he built nothing but illusions. He lived
in a world crafted by his own lies, and the most
elaborate of those lies came draped in white
dresses and new house keys.

He married five more times after he left our
mother.

As if one failed marriage hadn't taught him—or
anyone else—of what he was capable of. But each
time, he started fresh. He reinvented himself. He
smiled at the altar as if someone had wiped a clean
slate. Like he hadn't torn through the lives of a
wife and four children and left them in ruins.

Each new bride walked into his life hopeful.
And each one walked out damaged.

Four marriages ended in divorce. Predictably.
Quietly. Sometimes after explosive fights,

sometimes just through the slow erosion that happens when a man turns affection into ammunition. He knew how to charm, but not how to love. He knew how to impress, but not how to care. And eventually, even those who had once looked at him with soft eyes came to see what we had always known.

He would never change.

The fifth wife—the final one—didn't leave him

She stayed until his death.

She told us later, in whispers and broken glances, that she feared for her life. That she'd lie awake at night and wonder if she'd wake up to find him standing over her with rage in his eyes and revenge in his hands. She had lived with a knot of fear in her chest, the same knot our mother had carried, and the same one we, as his children, had learned to carry far too young.

But while these women came and went, often giving away houses and promises, they left my mother behind—in every sense of the word.

He left her in the same house he had once filled with violence, silence, and scorn. Not because she wanted to stay, but because he wanted her *stuck*. It wasn't just abandonment—it was punishment. She had been the one to raise his children. To cook, clean, and protect in a battlefield of a home. She had weathered his storms. She had survived. And he hated her for that.

So, while he handed keys to new wives, bought homes with fresh paint and manicured lawns, he made sure our mother sat in the wreckage. He kept the house in her name, maybe to keep a string of control wrapped around her, maybe just to be cruel.

The message was clear: *You stay here. You stay with what I left you with.*

And he sold off the rest.

The lake house he once promised to my brother. Gone.
The small plot of land that was supposed to be passed down to us kids? Sold to a stranger.
The family heirlooms, the things with memories tied to them? Traded or discarded without a second thought.

He lived only for himself, clinging to his lies like lifelines. He told people he was a good father. A war hero. A devoted husband. He rewrote history with every introduction, painting himself as a man wronged, a victim of bad luck and an ungrateful family.

But we knew the truth.
We had lived it.

And the saddest part is, he *could* have been better.
He had choices. He had chances.
But he burned bridges rather than built them.

He chose women who didn't yet know his past
because fresh eyes didn't yet flinch. He was driven
to choose new homes to escape the ghosts haunting
his old ones. He chose the mirror over the
window—always more interested in his reflection
than in seeing the surrounding damage.

Each marriage was a mask. A new costume in a
play that never ended. But behind the curtain, he
was still the same man—angry, controlling,
dishonest. There's always someone to blame.
Never once willing to look in the mirror long
enough to see what we saw: a man who had lost
everything because he didn't know how to keep
anything.

And yet, through it all, our mother endured.

Necessity, not choice, kept her rooted. In the
home, echoing with slammed doors and broken
promises, she raised us. To feed her family, she
wore out. With each act of love, she mended the
walls and our hearts. After that, she chose not to

marry again. She never ran away from her responsibilities. She just kept going.

While he played house with new brides, she built a proper home with what little she had left.

And we watched. His favoritism toward strangers stung us. We felt the cold shoulder of being children that no longer fit into the new life he was creating repeatedly.

But we also learned resilience.

We learned to value things beyond monetary worth.
We learned to make memories that didn't need a price tag.
We have come to understand that love is not measured by the frequency of saying "I do." It's about what you do when someone needs you most.

By the time he died, the damage had already been done. The card house had fallen. Gone were the wives. The children had grown. His own actions left him with an echo—a life full of noise and nothingness.

He thought love was something you bought.
He believed that manipulating loyalty was possible.
He thought family was optional.

But he was wrong.

In the end, all he had were stories—ones he
twisted to make himself the hero.

But we who lived it know the truth.
And the truth is what we carry forward.
Not his lies.
Not his homes.
Not his name.

Just the truth—and the strength it took to rise from
it.

Chapter 46

I didn't go

Truth…

I didn't go to my father's funeral.

People say that funerals are for the living, for
closure, for last goodbyes. But what do you say
goodbye to when someone was never truly there to
begin with? What do you grieve when what you
lost was never love—but safety, trust, and
innocence?

There are those who tried to guilt me into going.
"It's your father," they said.
As if blood alone should bind me to a pew, forcing
me to swallow memories I've choked on for years.

But I didn't go.

Because honoring someone at the end of their life
means something.
It's a ritual.
It's respect.

And my father had spent a lifetime proving he
didn't deserve either.

He wasn't a good man. Not to us. Maybe to others he was charming, or witty, or full of tall tales that made people laugh. But to his children, he was something else entirely. The sound of his keys in the door sent shivers down our spines. He was the rage that silenced rooms. He was a voice that tore down, never built up. The man who bought new homes for strangers while leaving his family behind in the wreckage he created.

He was a pistol at my brother's temple.
The shadows of our childhood.
The silence when we needed protection the most.

And so, when the day came—the service, the burial, the artificial hush of a funeral home—I stayed home.

Not out of hate.

But out of honesty.

Because attending would've been a lie. To sit there, to bow my head, to listen to sanitized eulogies that painted him as a misunderstood man, a father of five, a complicated soul—it would've been betrayal. Not to him, but to *myself*.

He had five children. But he didn't raise five children. He damaged them. Fractured them. Left them hungry, emotionally, and physically. And

253

when he finally left, he didn't look back. He moved on. Married again. And again. And again. He built houses with other women while leaving us stuck in a home full of ghosts.

What kind of father does that?

People don't like it when you speak ill of the dead. They say, "Let him rest." But where were those voices when I was a child, afraid to sleep at night? Where were they when he tore our mother down with words designed to make her feel small? When he beat us down not with fists, but with control, cruelty, and silence?

Let him rest?

He rested his whole life while others carried the weight.

No, I didn't go.

Instead, I sat outside that day. The sky was wide and quiet. I breathed in the air as if it owed me something. Like the world had shifted slightly, and I could finally accept space without him watching from across the street or waiting to reappear in the middle of the night.

I thought about all the moments I needed a father and didn't have one. The moment I achieved something small but significant and looked around, hoping, just once, that maybe he'd say he was proud.

He never did.

So, I didn't go to say goodbye.

I'd said goodbye long before they lowered his casket into the earth.
I said goodbye the day he chose a new family over the one he already had.
I said goodbye when he held a knife to my throat.
I said goodbye when he came into our house with a pistol and left our mother shaking.
I said goodbye every time I locked a door—not to keep the world out, but to keep his memory at bay.

There was nothing left to mourn.
What died wasn't a father.
It was the hope that he would ever become one.

I don't feel guilty for not being there.

I feel free.

Free from grieving: No longer performing grief. No longer: no more pretending. Free from the lie that just because someone helped create you, they earned your tears. He didn't.

I've shed many tears in my life.
But not at his funeral.
Not him.

Grief is sacred. And he didn't get that from me,
too.

Forgiveness heals people. Others by letting go.
I chose both.
I forgave myself for wanting his love.
And I forgave him for not giving it.

I let go of the past and moved on with my future.

It took years. Decades, really. But I learned that
sometimes not showing up is the bravest thing you
can do. Sometimes the only way to honor your
truth is to stay home, breathe in peace, and let the
world keep spinning without pretending someone
was more than they really were.

He left me long before he died.
And I left him the moment I realized my worth
didn't depend on his ability to see it.

So, no—I didn't go.

Chapter 47

The Butterfly

Transformation…

It wasn't just a tattoo. Not to me.

It was a symbol. It's a declaration. A turning point etched onto my skin with ink and intention. A butterfly—delicate, quiet, but impossibly strong—marking the moment I claimed myself back from everything that had tried to break me.

I didn't get it on a whim. It wasn't about rebellion or fashion or following a trend. It was about survival. About freedom. About becoming.

For most of my life, my body never really felt like mine. It had been a battlefield, a vessel of fear and silence. I grew up flinching, hiding, enduring. My father controlled everything—our movements, our food, our thoughts, our stories. Furthermore, in the worst of times, it felt like even our skin didn't belong to us. It belonged to his rage. To his manipulation. To the systems that failed us.

But the butterfly? That was mine.

I chose it because butterflies are born from confinement. They start in darkness, wrapped tight in a cocoon, dissolving into something unrecognizable before reshaping into beauty. That felt like me. Pain broke me down and reshaped me. But I had emerged.

Quietly.
Slowly.
But I had emerged.

On the day I got the tattoo, I was nervous. Not about the pain—I had survived worse. I was nervous because it felt like the last step. Like turning a page. Like sealing a promise. And there was something terrifying about believing I deserved to make that promise to myself.

I walked into the shop with my head held high, but my heart was racing. The buzzing sound of the needle was sharp and constant. The artist, a kind man with inked arms and gentle eyes, asked me where I wanted it.

"Here," I said, pointing by my hip bone.
Right where no one will see it but me.

He asked why a butterfly, and I paused.
Then I said, "Because I wasn't supposed to make it. And I did."

He nodded as if he understood more than I said aloud.

As the needle moved, I thought of the little girl I used to be. The one who hid behind doors. Who slept with one eye open? Who begged the universe to make it stop. I thought of how she learned to be small, to disappear, to survive in silence.

I thought of the teenage me, walking through hallways pretending I hadn't spent the night before listening to shouting through paper-thin walls. I thought of the girl who had to be an adult long before she was ready. Who carried shame that didn't belong to her, and pain that no one could see.

And I thought of my mom.
How she bore it all.
How she protected us even when she had nothing left in her.
How she never got a tattoo, never screamed at the sky, never broke down in front of us—because she was too busy being our anchor.

The butterfly burned into my skin.
Not painfully—but deeply.
With every pass of the needle, I felt lighter.

It wasn't erasing the past.
It was honoring it.

Each wing of the butterfly held weight. One fear I had let go. One for the freedom I was stepping into. It exhibited symmetry. Grace was clear. It was proof that I had changed—and was still changing.

When it was done, I looked in the mirror.
There it was.
Simple. Soft.
But it pulsed with everything I had lived through.

It was me.

I remember driving home afterward, my skin tender, the bandage pressed gently against my skin. The sun was setting, casting gold across the dashboard. I rolled the windows down, letting the wind tangle my hair, and — for the first time in a long time—I felt *free*.

Not the freedom that comes from running.
The kind that comes from standing still and finally feeling safe.

Later, I showed it to my daughter. She smiled and said, "That fits you."
And it did.
Because I wasn't a victim anymore.
I wasn't a prisoner of that house, that man, or those memories.

I was the girl who survived and still had the courage to fly.

Over time, the butterfly became more than a symbol.
It became a reminder.
On hard days, I'd run my fingers over it and whisper to myself, "You're still free."
On good days, I'd wear it proudly like a badge of honor, a quiet tribute to the journey I had taken.

I now smile—not the forced kind, but the real one—and say to myself:

"I lived."

That little inked on my hip carried more truth than any funeral speech ever could. It carried the story of a girl who saw monsters in daylight and learned to walk in the dark. Who grew up in chaos but chose peace. Who broke, and instead of remaining broken, became art.

I know I'm not done healing.
The past doesn't vanish with ink or years.
But now I have something permanent to hold on to.

Not pain.
Not shame.
Power.

The butterfly is mine.
And so is this life I built after him?

Chapter 48

The Four of Us

Unity...

There were four of us.

Four children raised in the same house, under the same roof, beneath the same heavy shadow. The same voices shaped us, the same silences, the same long nights where we listened for footsteps that meant trouble. And yet, somehow—miraculously—we all grew up. We all moved on.

But no one walks away from a burning house without scars.

We don't talk about the past much. We mention it in passing, like a bad dream we mostly forgot. A nod, a shrug, a quiet agreement that we survived it, so what more is there to say?

But it's there.

It's always there.

Lurking in the quiet corners of our minds, peeking out from behind family holidays and recent memories. Raised voices cause us to flinch. We carry the trauma without meaning to. Like dust in our lungs. Like gravity in our bones.

Still, we moved forward.

My oldest sister became a mother too early, maybe, but fiercely. She was the one who bore the weight before any of us even understood what we were living through. She tried so hard to protect us, even when she was just a child herself. The house across the street to the left, the abuse, the pain—it swallowed her because when it finally broke, it broke hard. The trauma scattered her in different directions for years. Drugs, rebellion, heartbreak. She became weak, and she was unable to stitch herself back together. Piece by piece. Her healing didn't look like ours. It wasn't as we hoped, and she was never the same. We talk little about what happened to her as a little girl, the things she saw and suffered. But I know what happened, and I carry her truth with me.

My brother ran away more than once. But running was for survival, not escape. When he finally got out for good, it was like watching a bird learn how to fly after being caged for so long. He helped people. Worked hard. Became someone others could count on. And in doing that, he found himself. He found freedom. He moved on, but not with bitterness. With quiet strength. And yet, now, and then, I still see it in his eyes—the way he zones out when someone mentions our father. The way he carries responsibility like a shield. He laughs more now. But pain carved his laughter.

My other sister—just a year older than me—had her own battles. She found her footing, in a horse she once trusted more than people, and later, in her children. Her life wasn't easy. The trauma followed her. But she kept going. She built something better than what we were born into.

And then there's me.

The youngest.

The one who watched, listened, absorbed everything. The one who held her breath through her childhood, waiting for the next blow—not a physical one always, but the kind that shattered you on the inside. I learned to be small. Not to be in the way. To keep the peace. And when it was finally over—when Dad was gone when the chaos quieted—I found my voice. I wrote. To speak. To breathe again.

I got a tattoo—a butterfly— not for beauty, but for survival. A symbol of transformation. A declaration of freedom. It was my line in the sand: I am not what he did. I am not in the past. I am not a prisoner.

But I still remember.

We all do.

We remember birthdays that ended in tears. Nights spent hiding. The constant feeling that something bad could happen at any moment. We remember the hunger. The fear. The silence that screamed louder than any shout.

We remember the pistol and the knife.
The threats.
The promises he made.
The houses he left us behind in.
The food we didn't have.
The warmth we craved.

And yet—we smile now.

But healing isn't erasing.

It's living *with* the memory and not letting it rule you.

It's knowing where you came from and choosing to build something better, anyway.

We don't gather often, Life pulls us in different directions. But when we do, there's an unspoken understanding. A knowing glance. A shared language that only we speak. We survived the

same war, even if we came out with different
wounds. And when we laugh together now, it's
real. It's earned. It's beautiful because it's not built
on pretending everything was fine—but on
knowing it wasn't and still choosing joy.

Sometimes late at night, I wonder how we made it.
How four children born in the same storm-built
lives that look nothing like where we started.
We're not perfect. Despite: despite it all, we still
have our moments. We still carry pieces of it all.

But we've escaped.

He did not define us.

Our resilience defines us.

By the way we keep showing up—for ourselves,
for each other, for our children.

We learned to love, even though no one showed us
how.

We reached for hope in the dark.

Yes, the memories still live within the backs of our
minds.
But now we live in the light.

Chapter 49

Now They're Free

Peace...

We've lost them both now—our mother, and our oldest sister.

And there are still days when it doesn't feel real. Maybe they're just in the next room. Maybe we'll hear Mom's voice calling us in for dinner, or our sister's laughter rising from the yard. But that's memory talking, not truth.

The truth is—they're gone.

And yet, there's a quiet peace in it too.

Because if anyone deserved rest, it was they.

Our mother was a woman who endured more than most people could ever understand. Fear, like lingering smoke, permeated the house where she raised us. She stayed not because she didn't want to leave, but because she didn't know how—or where we'd go if she did. She made impossible choices with what little she had. And somehow, in all of it, she gave us enough love to carry forward.

Not perfect love. Not fairytale love. But love in its most honest, battered form: survival, sacrifice, and presence.

She had an eighth-grade education, and yet she taught us the most important lessons of all. Maintaining momentum: How can you keep going? Loving fiercely, even in darkness, is the question. How to protect each other. How to fight for peace when the world offers none.

She gave everything.

She stayed when it hurt.
She fought without weapons.
She loved without rest.

And now she rests.

When she died, it felt like the roof had finally caved in. She had been our shelter, even when she was barely standing herself. But as the dust settled, a strange thought crept in. Maybe this is what freedom finally looks like—for her.

She doesn't have to be strong anymore.
She doesn't have to carry the weight.
She doesn't have to endure.

She is free.

Our oldest sister followed not long after. Her road was different but also paved with pain. She was the first to witness the full extent of what he was capable of. The first to be let down. The first to be broken. And the first to protect the rest of us.

She was our shield—sometimes our second mother, when Mom couldn't be in all places at once. At too young of an age, too young, she knew too much. She bore scars no child should bear. And for years, it haunted her. She struggled. She fought demons we couldn't see. Addiction, heartbreak, anger that had nowhere to go but inward.

But she had joy, too. Laughter that was wild and bright when it came. A love of animals, of music, and of the few things in the world that made her feel seen. And she had us. Even when she pushed us away, we never stopped being her siblings. We never stopped loving her.

She loved her children with everything she had. And even in her lowest moments, she wanted better for them than she ever had for herself. That mattered. That was her attempt to rewrite the story.

When she passed, it hit differently. There was a shock. There was pain. But there was also—

again—that strange whisper: *Now she doesn't have to fight anymore.*

She fought throughout her entire life.
She deserved peace.

And maybe now she's finally found it.

We grieve for them both, deeply. In different ways. In waves that come out of nowhere, smelling something that reminds us of them, or seeing a picture we'd forgotten, or hearing a song that breaks us wide open. Grief isn't linear. It's a loop. A rhythm. A silent song only we hear.

But in our grief, we hold gratitude.

Because we *had* them.

Because in a world that tried to take everything from us, we had their love—even if it was messy, even if it was hard.

And now, even in their absence, they are with us.

Mom is in the way we hold our children a little longer at night.
She's in the way we stretch every dollar to make things work.
She's in our strength—the kind that doesn't make noise but never breaks.

Our sister is in the songs we hum without
realizing.
She's in the moments we choose compassion, even
when it's hard.
She's in our fire, our protectiveness, our fierce
belief that trauma ends with us.

They are gone, yes.
But they are also free.

And maybe that's what gives us the strength to
keep going. To continue the healing, they began.
To build the lives they dreamed of but couldn't
quite reach.

We still cry.
We still ache.
We still wish for one more day.

But we also smile.
We laugh.
We live.

Because they did.
Because they loved us enough to make it possible.

There are three of us siblings still standing. And
though we've lost two of the most important
people in our story, we carry them with us in every
chapter. We honor them not by living in the past,

but by building futures filled with light, safety, and truth.

We still have harsh memories. We always will. But those memories don't own us. They sit in the back of our minds, quieter now. Because love—genuine love—has spoken louder.

And in the silence after loss, we hear something we didn't expect:

Peace.

Not because it doesn't hurt.

But now finally, they are free.

Chapter 50

The Light We Chose

Hope...

We've carried so much. The past, the quiet, the shattered pieces. Indistinguishable mornings resulted from sleepless nights. The years that left bruises on our memories, even if they never touched our skin.

But this isn't just a story of pain.

This is a story of *what came after.*

Because somewhere along the way, we learned to breathe again. To laugh again. To *live*—not just survive.

It didn't happen all at once. Healing never does. It came in moments. Small and quiet successes that were not always noticeable. The phone rang. A shared meal. Remembering a birthday. A smile that didn't feel forced

We weren't just siblings—we were survivors.

We didn't need many words back then. Just a glance. A shift in the air. We could read each other without speaking.. We didn't talk about what was happening—not really—but we always showed up for each other. Every time.

There were nights when it felt like the walls of our house would cave in. When yelling turned to crashing. When I'd pull the covers over my head and wish I could disappear. But I wasn't alone. Not really. Because I knew—no matter how dark the night got—my siblings were, awake like me, carrying the same weight.

We got through it together.

So many things tried to pull us apart. Violence. Distance. Heartbreak. But we're still here.

Because when you walk through fire with someone, and they never let go of your hand—you don't forget that. You don't take that for granted.

You hold on tighter...

Epilogue

The Light That Stayed...

Some stories live quietly in the shadows, buried beneath years of silence, tucked behind smiles that carry too much weight. Ours was one of those stories. For so long, it felt safer to keep it hidden— to pretend that pain wasn't part of our past, that fear didn't tuck us into bed at night, and that our scars weren't still aching beneath the surface. But silence never healed us. And hiding never set us free.

So, we told the truth.

We told it for the sister who was kidnapped and never looked at the world the same.
For the boy who packed a bag with trembling hands and ran because the house wasn't safe.
For the sister who learned far too young that some wounds aren't visible, but they cut just as deep.
And for every child who sat on a quiet porch step, waiting for someone to notice they were not okay.

Our story is not easy. There were monsters in our neighborhood and ghosts in our own home. We grew up dodging more than just trouble—we dodged truths, fists, broken promises, and the long shadows cast by adults who should have protected us. We lived in houses with locked doors and even tighter hearts. But through it all, we never stopped hoping that one day, someone would listen. That someone would care.

If you're holding this book, maybe you are that someone. Maybe you're a survivor, too. Or maybe you're the friend, the teacher, the neighbor, or the stranger who wants to understand. Whoever you are, thank you for stepping into our truth. Thank you for not turning away.

The journey of writing this was not just about documenting pain—it was about reclaiming power. Every chapter is a brick we pulled from the walls we once built around ourselves. Every memory we unearthed is a thread we wove into something stronger than sorrow—into resilience, into courage, into hope. And at the heart of it all, what stayed steady. Even in the darkest nights, we had each other. My siblings and I—four lights flickering, but never out.

We grew up too fast. We lost too much. But somehow, we held on. Not just for survival, but to each other. We laughed when we could. We cried when we had to. And we built a bond that the worst of this world could not destroy. That's what I hope lingers when the last page turns: not just the pain, but the love. Not just the trauma, but the triumph.

Our story doesn't end in bitterness. It ends in choosing light—again and again. We chose forgiveness, even when we didn't feel it yet. We chose healing, even when it hurt. We chose to tell the truth, even when it trembled in our hands.

And now, we choose to give this story to you.

Because maybe, like us, you've been afraid to speak. Maybe you've lived in a house like ours. Maybe you've felt the sting of betrayal or the ache of abandonment. Maybe no one ever told you that what happened to you wasn't your fault. So let me say it clearly now: *It wasn't your fault.* You deserved safety. You deserved love. You deserved to be protected.

And you still do.

You are not broken. You are becoming. You are not alone. You are seen. And even if your story started in darkness, it doesn't have to end there.

We are proof of that.

Today, we live differently. We love differently. We parent differently. We broke a cycle that tried to break us. And we dream—something we once thought was impossible. We carry our past, yes, but we also carry a future that is softer, safer, and filled with the kind of peace we used to pray for.

Writing this book was like opening a wound—but in the light, wounds begin to heal.

To the reader who cried with us, thank you.
To the survivor who saw their own story in ours, you are brave.
To the person still trapped in silence, your voice matters.
To the sibling trying to stay close, even when life pulls hard—keep showing up for each other.
That's what my brother and I have done. Through every season, through every storm, we held fast. Because love like that? It doesn't let go.

Maybe one day, we'll meet—maybe in a bookstore, maybe through a letter, maybe just in spirit—but I hope you know this: you are part of our story now. Your hope keeps ours alive. Your healing makes ours deeper.

This book may close, but our hearts stay open.

We told our story because we had to.
We shared our pain so it wouldn't win.
And we offer our truth as a kind of map—one that might help someone else find their way out, too.

No matter where you come from, no matter how dark the road has been, there is always a light ahead.

Sometimes, that light is family.
Sometimes, it's a friend.
Sometimes, it's a book that dares to tell the truth.

So here's the truth.

Here's to the ones who survived.

Here's to the ones still trying.

And here's to all the places we called home—because even the broken ones made us who we are.

Thank you for walking this journey with us.

With both our hearts,
L.K. Menzies & R.D. Peterson

www.ingramcontent.com/pod-product-compliance
Lightning Source LLC
Chambersburg PA
CBHW071630140626
46555CB00022B/2045